Population, P and Movement

Series editor
Stuart Currie
Curriculum Manager: Humanities, Margaret Glen-Bott School, Nottingham

Geoffrey Brookes
Deputy Headteacher, Easingwold School, North Yorkshire

Claire Jones
Adviser of Geography, Wombwell High School, Barnsley

Peter McLeod
Acting Deputy Headteacher, High Green School, Sheffield

John Morris
General Inspector: Humanities, Nottinghamshire LEA

Richard Nicholls
formerly Head of Geography, City School, Sheffield

Collins Educational
An imprint of HarperCollins *Publishers*

LOCATION MAP

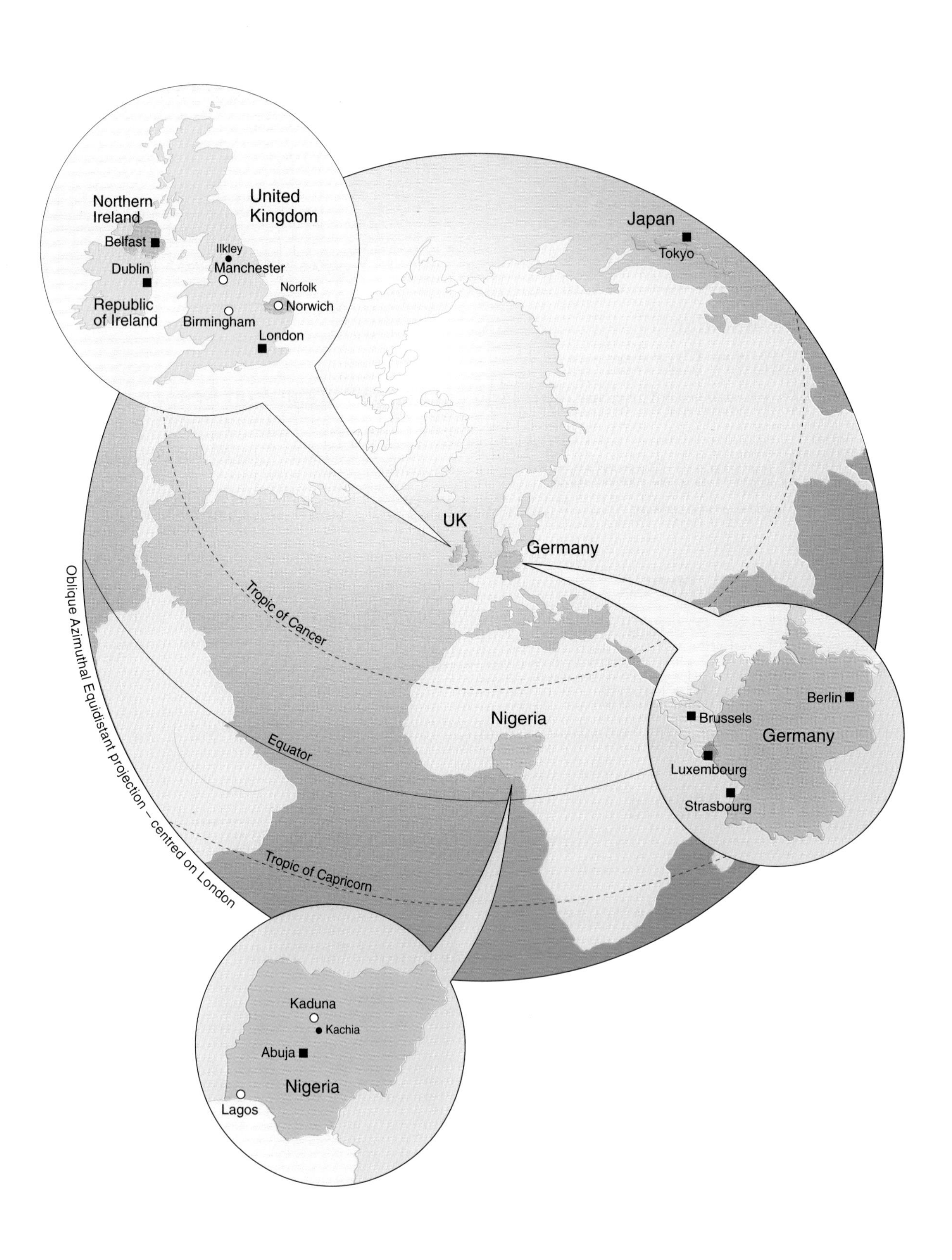

CONTENTS

1·1 GLOBAL POPULATION AND RESOURCES

Rapid population growth is placing great pressure on the world's resources. What is the impact of this growth on the environment and how is this likely to affect world development? How might people respond?

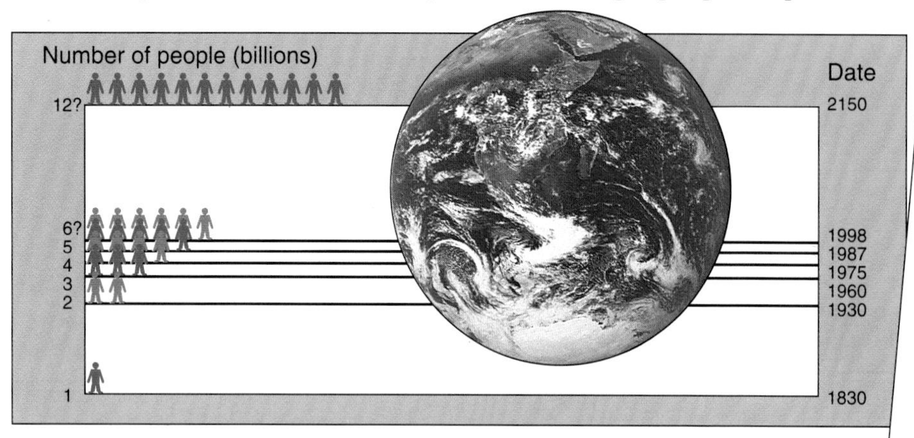

Source A Population growth – a threat to humankind?

Yesterday saw the start of the 1994 United Nations conference on population, the environment and development.

Representatives from many nations are meeting to discuss increasing concerns about world population growth and the use and misuse of resources.

The aim of the conference is to influence governments over their responsibilities for the needs of present and future generations.

- Between 1990 and the end of the twentieth century, an extra one billion people will live on the Earth.
- The world population will increase into the twenty-first century.
- The world population will double in forty years.
- Eighty per cent of the world's resources are consumed by 25 per cent of its population.
- World population growth is slowing down.
- The current global population has reached five billion.
- Life expectancy is increasing across the world.
- Migration can lead to population growth.
- Population growth in some countries is threatening ECONOMIC DEVELOPMENT.
- Population growth declines with economic development.

Source B Ten statements about the world's population: true or false?

1 Study Source A.
a Draw a line graph to show the rate of world population growth.
b Write a sentence describing what your graph shows.
c What will be the impact of this population change on:
• people, • the environment, • resources, • development?

2 Work with a partner. Read Source B.
a Write down the statements that you think are true.
b Compare your statements with another group. Justify your answers.

3 Working in a group, study Sources C, D and E. Describe the population–resource relationships shown in each photograph using the following headings:
• Area of land • Number of people and buildings
• Amount and type of resources being used.

Population – resource relationships

Source C A rural environment, UK

Source D A changing environment, near Port Harcourt, Nigeria

Worlds apart

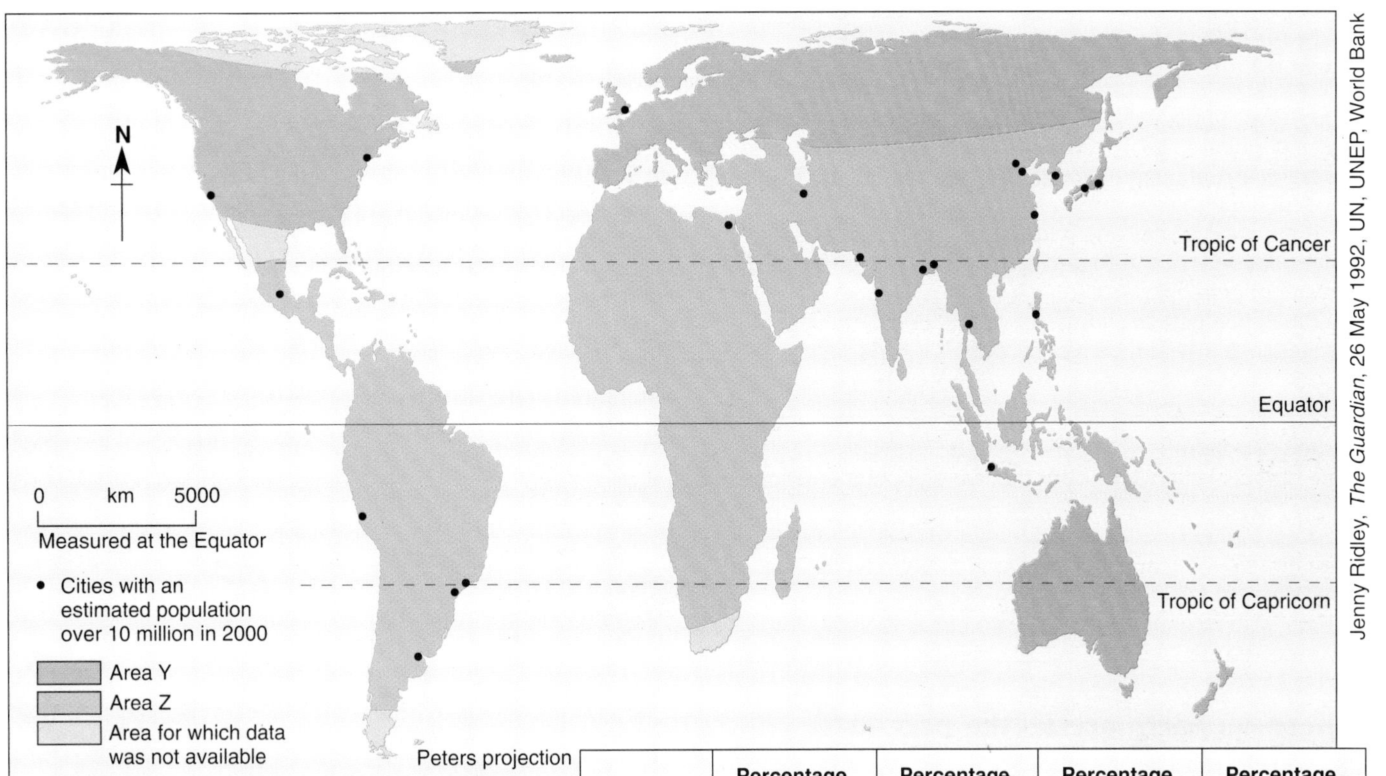

	Percentage of world population	Percentage of world energy consumption	Percentage of world industry	Percentage of world income
Area Y	25		86	
Area Z		20		15

NOTE: Assume area Y + area Z = 100%

Source F Global inequalities in the distribution of people and resources, 1990

Source E An urban environment, Tokyo, Japan

4 Using Source F and an atlas:
a State the area, Y or Z, where each of the following countries is found: Germany, Japan, Mexico and Nigeria.
b Name two other countries in area Y and two in area Z.

5 **a** Copy and complete the table, Source F.
b Draw four graphs to show the differences between areas Y and Z.
c Comment on the differences shown in your pie charts.
d Choose suitable names to describe areas Y and Z.
e *The population of area Z is growing faster than area Y. What will be the impact of this on people living in these areas?*

6 On a copy of Source F and using an atlas:
a Name the 23 cities marked.
b Make a table to show the cities in areas Y and Z.
c How many of these cities are in:
• area Y, • area Z?
d Suggest a reason to explain why there are more large cities in one area than the other.
e Suggest why so many of the cities marked on the map are located on or near to the coast.

1·2 The impact of population change

The number of people in the world continues to increase. The rate of population growth varies from one country to another. The fastest global population growth was in the late 1960s. Since then the rate of growth has slowed down.

Population trends and patterns of growth depend on differences between birth and death rates, as well as on the movement of people.

Small percentage changes in population can mean large changes in actual numbers of people.

Crude BIRTH RATE
The number of live births per thousand population each year.
Crude DEATH RATE
The number of deaths per thousand population each year.
NATURAL INCREASE
Crude birth rate minus crude death rate.

1 Study Source A.
a Write two or three sentences to describe the distribution of the world's population in 1990.
b Use the predicted data for the year 2000 to draw a pie chart.
c In which continents will populations:
• increase, • decrease?

2 **a** Copy and complete Source B.
b Use your completed table to explain predicted differences in the distribution of the world's population (Source A).

3 Study Source C.
a Describe the changes in global birth and death rates between 1965 and 1990.
b What effect will these changes have on the rate of global population growth?
c In pairs, brainstorm some of the reasons for changes in crude birth and death rates.

Where on earth are all the people?

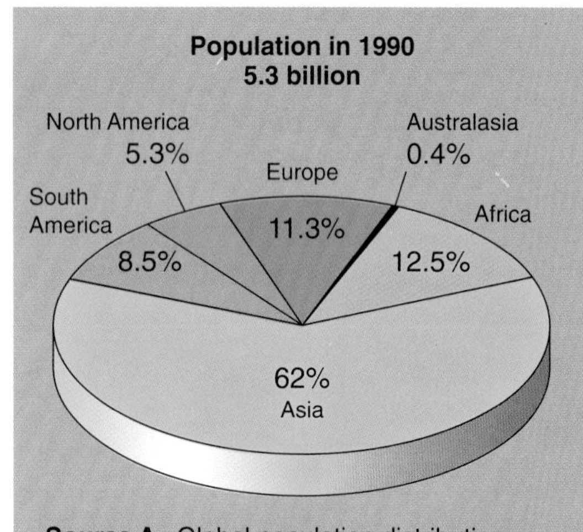

Estimated population in 2000
6.2 billion

Continent	Percentage share
Africa	14.0
Asia	62.5
North America	4.8
South America	8.5
Europe	9.8
Australasia	0.4

Source A Global population distribution

Country	Crude birth rate (per 1000 population)	Crude death rate (per 1000 population)	Natural increase of population	Percentage increase of population
Nigeria	43	14	29	2.9
Mexico	27	5		2.2
UK	13	11	2	
USA	17			0.8
Germany	11	11		
Japan		7	4	

Source B Population changes in selected countries, 1990

Birth rate
per 1000 population
1965 35
1990 26

Death rate
per 1000 population
1965 13
1990 9

Source C Global birth and death rates. The sculpture of birth is by Gustav Vigland and is part of a display on life in the Vigland Park, Oslo

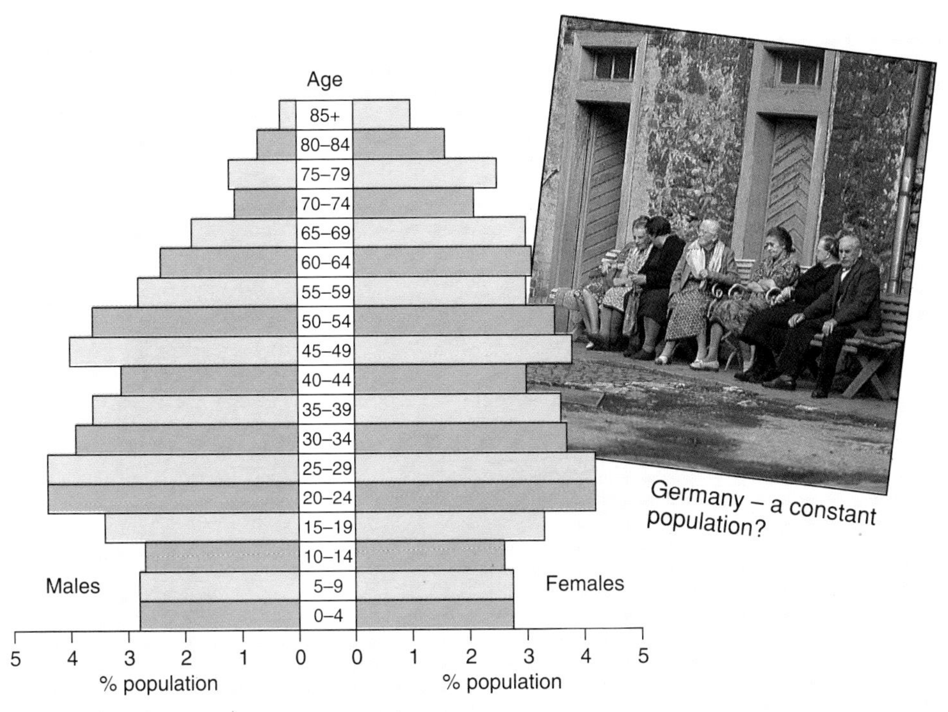

Source D Germany: population structure, 1990

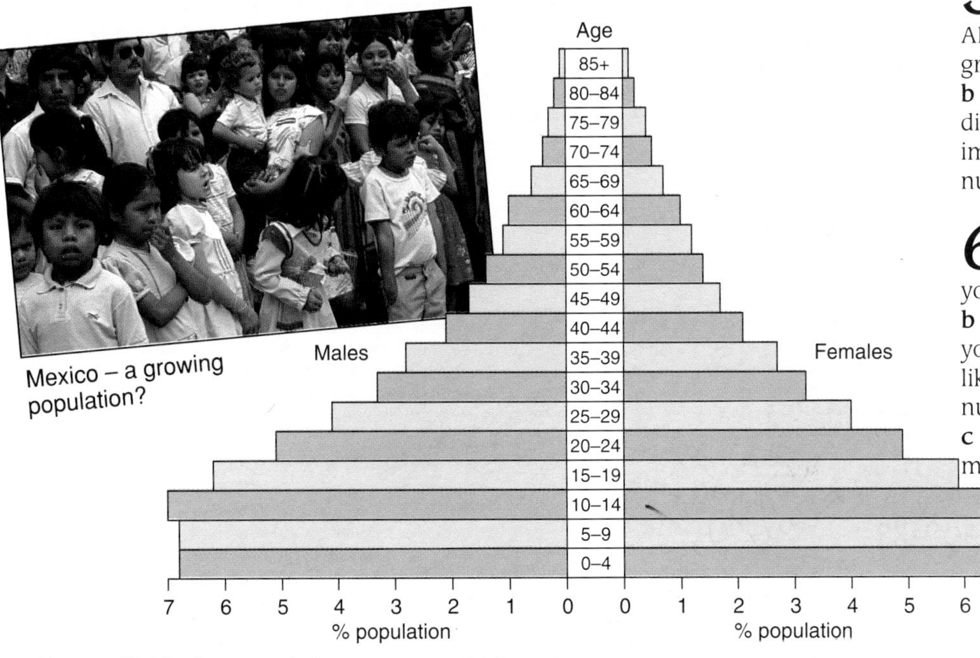

Source E Mexico: population structure, 1990

4 Study Sources D and E.
a Describe the shape of each country's population pyramid.
b Copy and complete the table below.

Age	Mexico	Germany
0 – 14		
60+		

c Use Source B to explain the differences between the population structure of Germany and Mexico.
d For each country, write a paragraph suggesting what your table tells you about:
- *life expectancy*
- *the number of people the working population has to support*
- *the demands for health care and education.*

Threats to the population

5 Study Source F.
a Explain how diseases such as AIDS can affect population growth and numbers.
b Suggest three factors other than disease which could have the same impact on population growth and numbers. Explain your answer.

6 Work in a group.
a Choose one of the three factors you have described.
b Find out all you can about the factor you have chosen and the effect it is likely to have on population growth and numbers of people.
c Present your findings as a wall-mounted display.

Source F AIDS – a threat to population growth and numbers?

2 million people in Asia could die of AIDS by the year 2000

500 000 Europeans are HIV positive

ZAMBIA DIES IN DAILY AIDS EXPLOSION

Freddie Mercury, lead singer with rock band Queen, dies of AIDS

2·1 LEAVING HOME

Pro-communist demonstration, Moscow

Each day thousands of people throughout the world leave their homes and move to a new life. Why does this happen? What is the impact of this migration on people and the places to which they move?

Managing a refugee crisis

Many MIGRANTS claim to be REFUGEES. The United Nations says that refugees must demonstrate that they have fled from persecution or fear. To be poor is not enough – economic refugees have no rights of asylum.

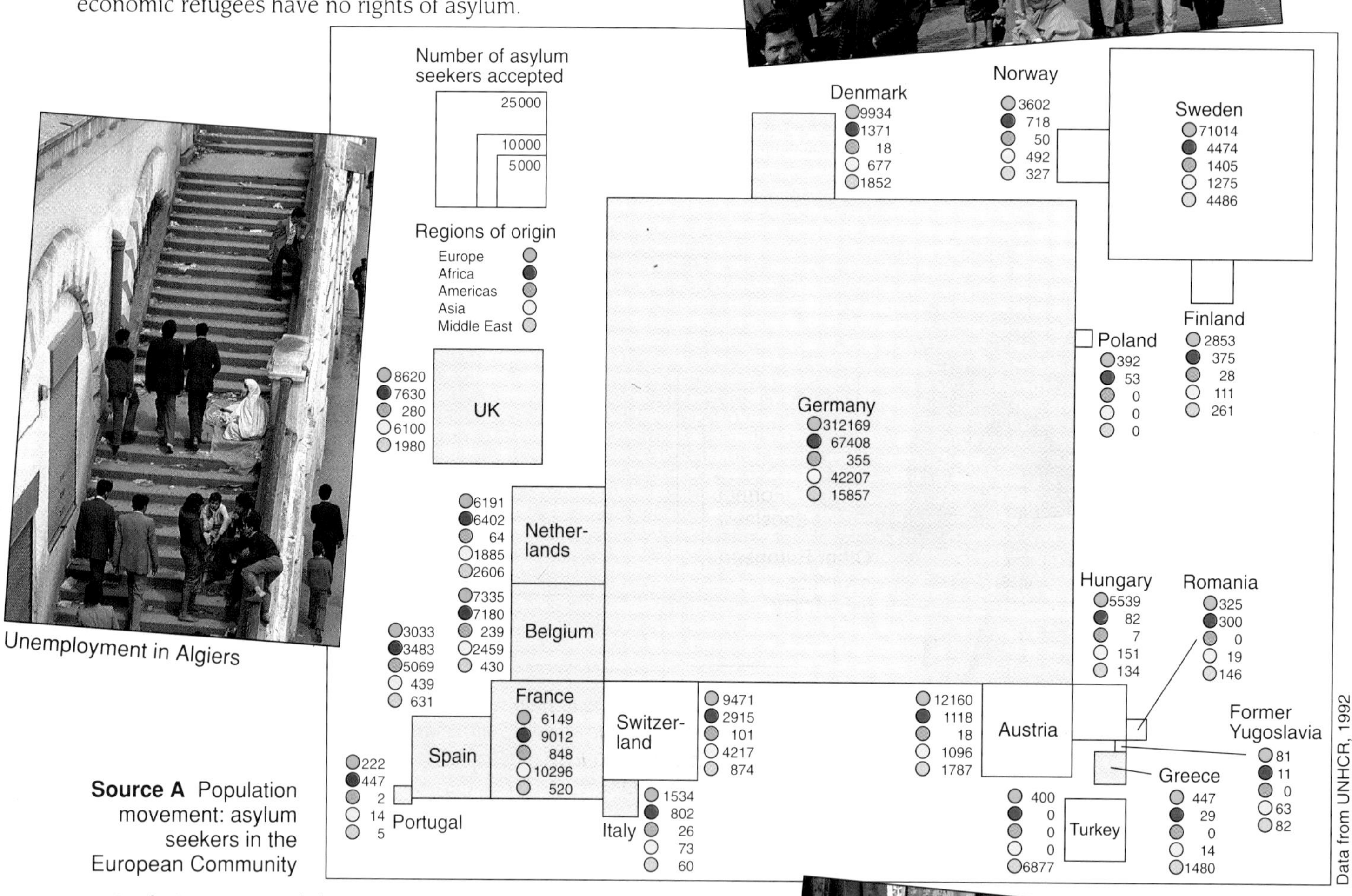

Unemployment in Algiers

Source A Population movement: asylum seekers in the European Community

1 Study Source A and the text.
a Which countries accepted
• the most, • the fewest asylum seekers in 1992?
b Name, in rank order, the five *EC* countries which accepted the greatest number of asylum seekers in 1992.
c For the five countries chosen in **b**, calculate the total number of asylum seekers from each of the five areas. Where have most asylum seekers come from?
d Suggest reasons to explain the movements of people between these places.

2 Imagine you are one of the people shown in the photographs. You are interviewed by a journalist. She asks you: • 'Why are you leaving your home?' • 'Where are you going to?' • 'Why have you chosen this country?' Write down your reply to each question.

Civil war in Bosnia and Herzegovina

The unwanted migrants of fortress Europe

Germany curbs immigration

New laws create Fortress Europe

10 000 demonstrate against changes in the law

Germany spends £4 billion per year on migrants

Source B German immigration laws tighten

On 26 May 1993, the German government voted in strict, new laws designed to reduce the number of IMMIGRANTS. Before this, Germany had the most relaxed immigration laws in Europe. Around 900 000 people annually crossed its borders. The new laws were the result of public pressure. In a poll just before the decision, 70 per cent of Germans felt that their country could no longer take in vast numbers of foreigners. They were worried that the German economy would not support increasing numbers of people.

Origins of non-EC migrants into Germany

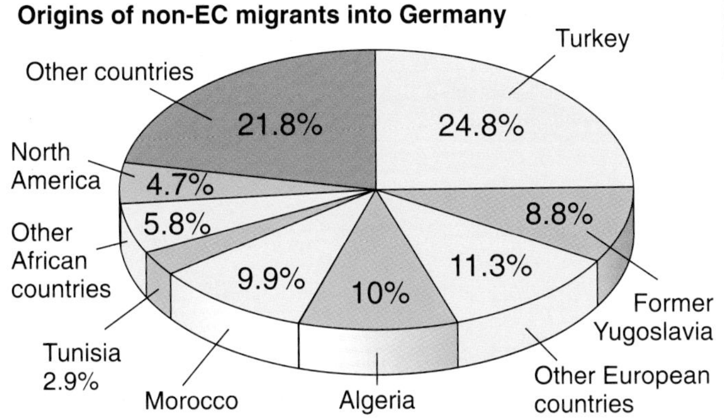

Turkey 24.8%
Former Yugoslavia 8.8%
Other European countries 11.3%
Algeria 10%
Morocco 9.9%
Tunisia 2.9%
Other African countries 5.8%
North America 4.7%
Other countries 21.8%

	Migrants of non-EC origin (% total pop. of region)	Migrants of EC origin (% total pop. of region)	GDP (% EC's total)
EC	2.5	1.5	100
Belgium	3.3	5.4	3.1
Denmark	2.3	0.5	1.7
France	3.8	2.8	18.7
Germany	5.7	2.1	21.3
Greece	1.2	1.0	1.7
Netherlands	3.1	1.1	4.7
Republic of Ireland	0.5	1.8	0.7
Italy	0.4	0.2	18.3
Luxembourg	0	28.2	0.2
Portugal	0.7	0.3	1.7
Spain	0.4	0.6	9.1
UK	1.8	1.4	18.8

Source C Percentage of foreign migrants in EC countries, 1990

Naturally, we would like to help refugees as much as possible. However, last year almost half a million looked for asylum in Germany. This couldn't last; the law had to tighten. I am trying to stop illegal immigrants, drug dealers and gun runners entering our country from the former Soviet Union and its neighbouring countries.

Source D Looking for illegal immigrants

Six central European States (Hungary, Poland, Austria, Slovenia, the Czech Republic and Slovakia) are concerned about Germany closing its borders. They are worried *they* will now receive far more refugees. They have plans for a new 'Iron Curtain' on their eastern and southern borders.

3 Study Source C.
a Which countries have the highest percentage of EC migrants? Suggest reasons to explain your answer.
b Which countries have the highest percentage of non-EC migrants?
c Is there a relationship between the percentage of migrants and GROSS DOMESTIC PRODUCT (GDP)? Give reasons for your answer.

4 **a** What do you think will be the effect of recent changes to Germany's immigration laws on the destinations of migrants into Europe?
b Why do you think some countries are worried by Germany's decision?

5 Use all the sources on these two pages.
a List the reasons why countries such as Germany have passed laws restricting the number of immigrants.
b *Many people in Germany are opposed to the new immigration laws. Suggest reasons to explain why some people think that refugees should be given asylum.*

2·2 Migration from the Republic of Ireland

Past patterns

During the past 150 years Ireland has experienced several large-scale migrations. After famine in the 1840s, the country's population fell by almost four million. EMIGRATION was one of the main reasons for this.

Source A Irish emigrants

A successful emigrant is welcomed home

St. Patrick's day celebrations, New York

Present trends

Present-day Ireland is divided into two countries, the Republic of Ireland and Northern Ireland. Since 1961, the Republic of Ireland's population has risen and migration into and out of the country has continued. Many emigrants are young and poorly qualified.

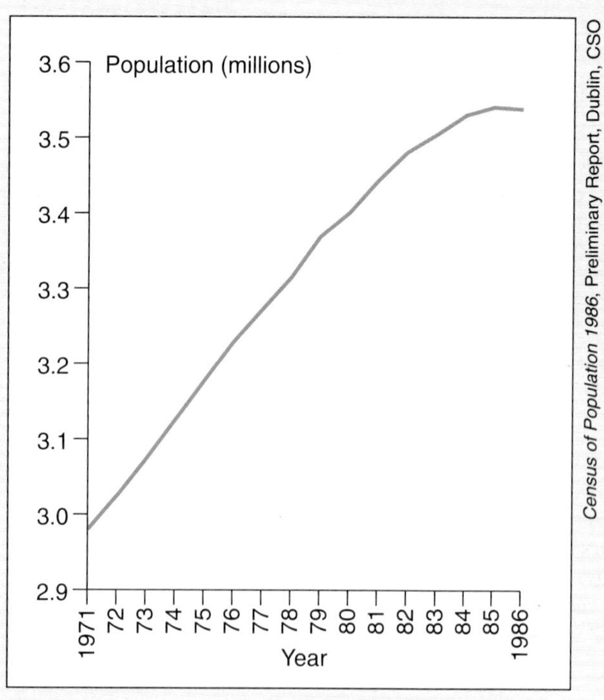

Source B Republic of Ireland: population change, 1971–86

Yearly change = NATURAL INCREASE ± net migration
Natural increase = BIRTH RATE − DEATH RATE
Net migration = immigration − emigration

Year	Yearly change (1000s)	Natural increase (1000s)	Net migration (1000s)
1972	+46	+35	+11
1973	+49	+35	+13
1974	+51	+35	+16
1975	+53	+34	+20
1976	+51	+35	+16
1977	+44	+34	+10
1978	+42	+35	+ 7
1979	+54	+38	+16
1980	+33	+41	− 8
1981	+42	+40	+ 2
1982	+37	+38	+ 1
1983	+24	+38	−14
1984	+25	+34	− 9
1985	+11	+31	−20
1986	− 3	+28	−31

Census of Population 1986, Preliminary Report, Dublin, CSO

Source C Republic of Ireland: components of population change, 1972–86

Patterns of migration

One of the main reasons for emigration was lack of work. Each year during the 1970s, the workforce grew by 20 000 but only 12 000 new jobs were created.

In the 1980s unemployment increased. A quarter of the workforce under the age of 25 had no job. During this period a new trend started: an increasing number of graduates emigrated. Graduates with science, engineering and computing qualifications are in demand by Europe's high-tech industries. High salaries and better career prospects attract the young, highly-qualified migrants. Graduate migration from the Republic of Ireland is a new trend and most emigrants have few qualifications.

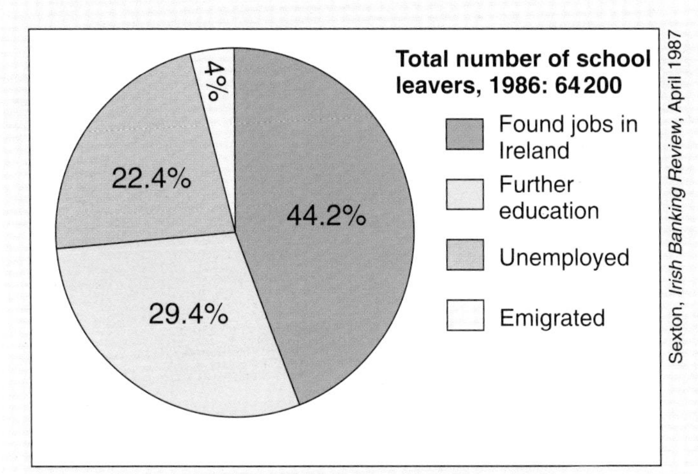

Source D Destination of Irish school leavers, 1986

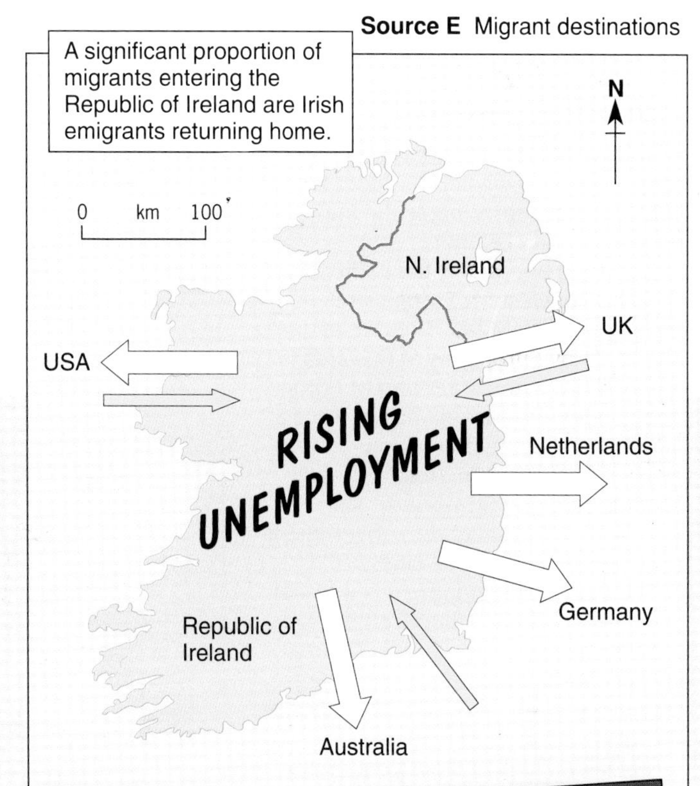

Source E Migrant destinations

Source F In 1985, 8.6 per cent of Irish business and commerce graduates, 37.6 per cent of engineers and 71.7 per cent of architects found work abroad

1 **a** Work with a partner. Make a list of reasons why people leave their homes and go to live in other places. Name a place people are leaving for each of the reasons you have given.
b Share your answers with the rest of the class. Add to your list new reasons given by others.
c Divide your list into two columns headed 'PUSH FACTORS' and 'PULL FACTORS'.

2 Read the text and look at Source A.
a Why do you think that so many people left Ireland in the nineteenth century?
b Name two groups of people who would have migrated.
c America is a popular destination of nineteenth century Irish migrants. Suggest one other.

3 Study Source B.
a Between which two years did the Republic of Ireland's population grow by the greatest amount?
b What happened to the population in 1986?
c Describe how the Republic of Ireland's population changed between 1971 and 1986.

4 Study Source C.
a On a copy of Source B, draw line graphs to show natural increase and net migration in the Republic of Ireland between 1972 and 1986.
b Use evidence from your graphs to explain why the population changed in 1986.
c How important has net migration been to population change in the Republic of Ireland? Justify your answer.

5 Study Source D.
a Calculate the percentage of school leavers in each of the four categories.
b Suggest why the percentage of emigrants who left school in 1986 is likely to increase over time.

6 Study Sources E and F.
a Suggest two reasons to explain why Irish emigrants are now more likely to choose Europe (including Britain) as a destination rather than the USA or Australia.
b Suggest what effects (political, economic, social, cultural) Irish communities might have on their host countries.

2·3 Migration to a European mega-city

The 'Blue Banana'

People are migrating to cities in the central areas of western Europe. Why does this happen? What is the impact on their QUALITY OF LIFE?

The 'Blue Banana' is the name given to a zone of western Europe stretching from London to Milan. The rate of migration by Europeans to this area is higher than to any other part of Europe. The London-Milan zone has become a mega-city of 80 million people. At its heart are three urban areas: Brussels, Luxembourg and Strasbourg. The European Community (EC) government is located in these three cities.

The European Parliament is unusual as it moves regularly between Brussels, Luxembourg and Strasbourg. The real cost of shuttling Eurocrats (politicians and civil servants) between the cities is not known. It is estimated at £1.82 billion, almost 5 per cent of the EC government's budget.

Before the development of the EC, the three cities had only a few luxury hotels; now there are many. When the European Parliament and the Council of Ministers meet there is not a room to be had.

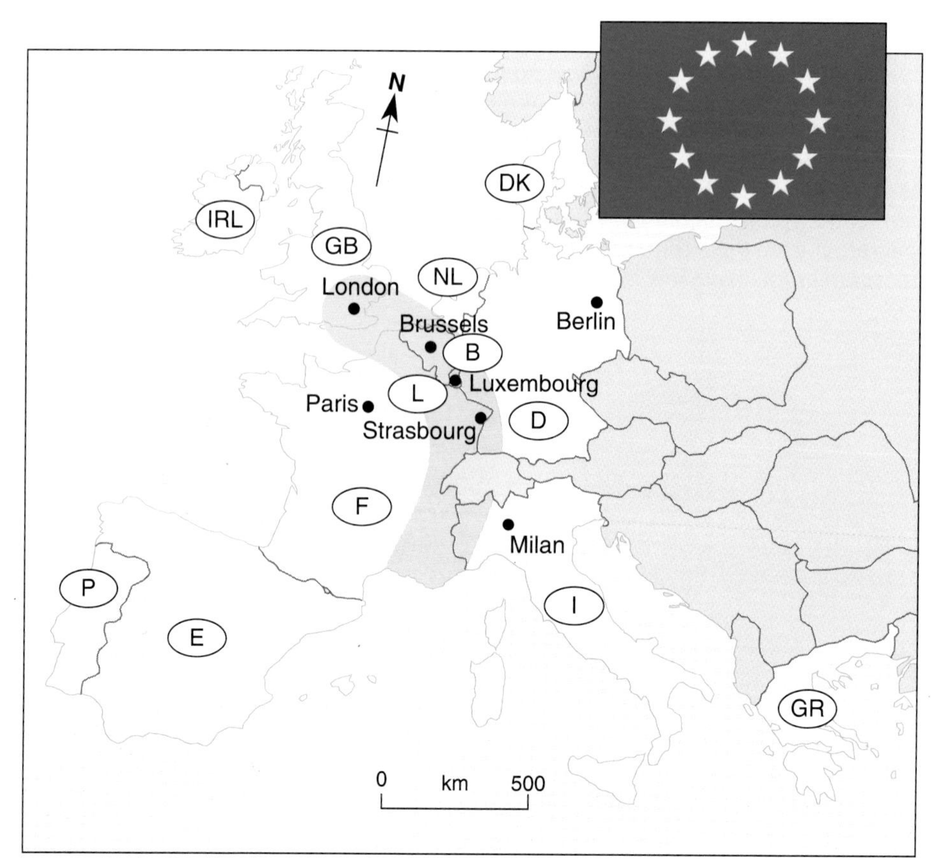

Source A The 'Blue Banana', a growth area in western Europe

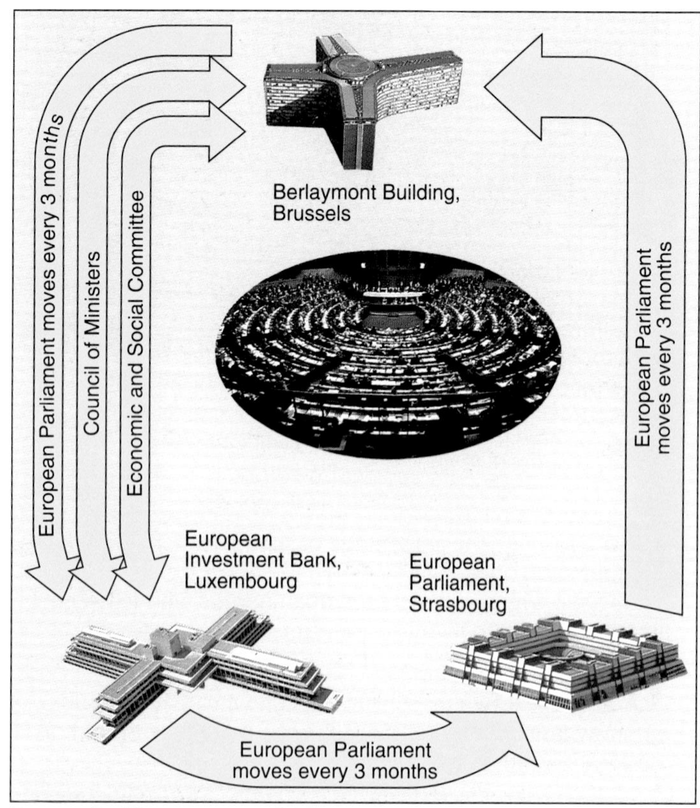

Source B The structure of EC government

	Permanent workers	Temporary workers
European Parliament	3 062	503
Council of Ministers	2 205	—
European Commission	16 426	749
European Court	693	101
European Audit Office	320	64
Total	**22 706**	**1 417**

Source C EC government employment, 1991

1 **a** Use Source A and an atlas to name the countries which belong to the EC.
b Which countries fall within the 'Blue Banana'?

2 Study Source B.
a Briefly explain how the European Parliament operates.
b In pairs, talk about the difficulties that might result from this structure. Share your views with the rest of the class.
c Write a short paragraph giving reasons why Brussels, Luxembourg and Strasbourg have become important.
d Use Sources B and C to draw a bar graph of EC employment in the three cities. Write a few sentences about any patterns of employment shown by your graph.
e Suggest five effects that the growth of the EC government might have had on the cities.

Living in the 'Blue Banana'

I work long hours and have a busy life which I enjoy. The salary and conditions of service are good, but living in Brussels is expensive. Commuting to EC offices in Luxembourg is a regular part of my work. I only work in Strasbourg when the Parliament meets there.

Source D Monique Smith, an EC interpreter

European Community: vacancies

Operations Manager for the International Office of the European Investment Bank.

Research and Development Engineer to advise the Council of Ministers. Computer skills and experience of international marketing required.

Interpreter at the European Parliament. Fluent in at least three EC languages.

Translator at the Council of Ministers. Desk–top publishing experience required.

Applicants should be graduates of an EC university with 8–12 years experience. Attractive salary and conditions of service by negotiation.

Application forms and passport sized photograph returned to:

European Parliament,
Recruitment Service,
Luxembourg.

Source E Job opportunities in the European Community

Source F European property

BRUSSELS: CAPITAL OF EUROPE

FOR SALE OR RENT: a range of luxury flats and houses located near to the city centre. Excellent access to EC offices. Properties also available in Luxembourg and Strasbourg.

LUXEMBOURG: SUPERB COUNTRY RESIDENCE

Luxury home set in own grounds (3500 m^2). Ideal for EC executive with large family. 6 bedrooms, 4 bathrooms, 2 double garages, swimming pool, snooker room and magnificent views across terraced lawns. Good motorway access to the airport and EC offices at Kirchberg. Offers over £650 000.

Contact: Euro–real Estate,
Rue des Bains, Luxembourg.

3 Study Sources D and E.

a List five different jobs carried out at EC government offices.

b In pairs, talk about and make notes on why EC jobs have high salaries.

4 Look at Source F.

a Why are houses in the centre of Brussels particularly suitable for Eurocrats?

b What problems might there be for people living near to the city centre?

c What is the likely impact of an increase in the number of highly paid Eurocrats on house prices in the 'Blue Banana'?

5 *Using all the sources, comment on the quality of life for those who work for the EC in the Brussels–Luxembourg region. Think about good and bad aspects of living and working there.*

3·1 GERMANY: ONE NATION . . .

Until recently, Germany was divided into two states: West and East. Political and economic change led to large-scale migration and the rebuilding of one nation. What are the impacts on people and places? How do people and governments respond?

28 August 1989: East German 'holiday-makers' crossed illegally into Austria. Others sought shelter in the West German embassies in Budapest, Prague and Warsaw.

THE BERLIN WALL, 1961–1989

9 November 1989: The flood of migrants became so great that the East German government removed its limits on visits and emigration to the West.

10 November 1989: Emigrants in front of the Brandenburg Gate, a historic symbol of a unified Germany.

11 November 1989: 'Wall Woodpeckers' break down the Berlin Wall, the symbol of a divided Germany.

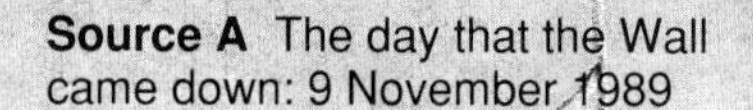

Source A The day that the Wall came down: 9 November 1989

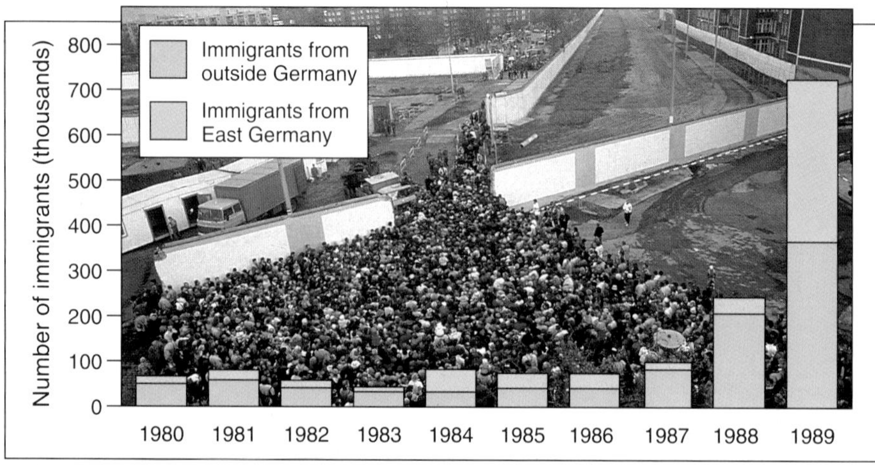

Source B IMMIGRATION into the former West Germany, 1980–9

1 Study Source A. Imagine that you are a reporter commenting on the events shown. Write a news report for radio, television or a newspaper. Your report should include what you have heard and seen.

2 Study Source B.
a In one or two sentences, describe the trends in MIGRATION.
b In which year did most migrants move from East to West Germany? Give reasons to explain your answer.
c In a small group, discuss why there was little migration from East Germany before this date.

One nation, many differences

I worry about a reunified Germany. The history of a single Germany is one of racism and shame.

Sabine Krauß, an East German

Today is a great day. The wall no longer divides us. This is the moment that we have awaited. For 28 years, we have hoped for this day. We Germans are now the happiest people in the world.

Walter Momper, Mayor of West Berlin, 10 November 1989

Source C Reunification: different views

Source D Shopping in West Berlin . . .

. . . and East Berlin

Differences in standards of living between East and West Berlin were an important influence behind reunification. Radio and television broadcasts told of the differences. These images and telephone calls between relatives on either side of the border increased levels of dissatisfaction.

In the late 1980s, East Germany suffered an increasing economic crisis. Lack of investment in new technology led to a fall in EXPORTS, national income and CONSUMER GOODS in the shops. When investment was made, it was too late to boost the state's dying economy.

3 Study Source C. Work in a small group.
a Using your school library, find out what historical events have led to the views in Source C.
b Present your findings to the rest of the class.

4 Study Source D. List the differences shown in the four photographs.

5 Use all the evidence on these two pages to help to explain the events leading to reunification.

3·2 Berlin: rebirth of a capital city

Divided and reunited

After the Second World War, Germany was divided into two states, and Berlin was separated into East and West Berlin. Reunification and the tearing down of the Berlin Wall has created new problems for the people of Germany.

Post-wall Berlin is still coming to terms with the task of uniting the two parts of the city. The two halves have been merging fast. More than 100 000 East Germans now work in former West Berlin.

In the eastern suburbs of Berlin there are West German banks and shops selling goods from Japan, Italy and France. Cars, buses and lorries cross the former border freely. Underground stations have been reopened. Despite these developments, Berlin still has Europe's largest inner-city wasteland.

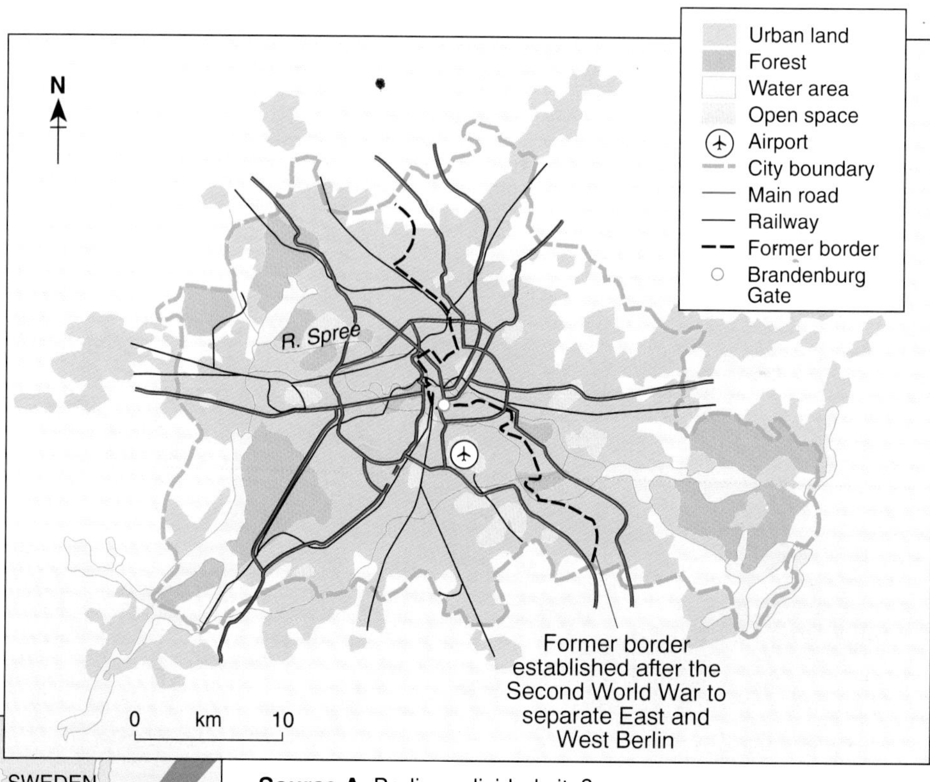

Source A Berlin: a divided city?

Date	Number of immigrants
1985–9	811 000
1990–4	696 000
1995–9	203 000
2000–4	114 000
2005–9	95 000
2010–14	83 000

Source B Actual migration of Germans to Berlin, 1985–9 and predicted migration 1990–2014

Future growth

Berlin is being transformed. New building is seen everywhere and over 6.5 million square metres of office space will have been built by 1995.

Redevelopment was stimulated by the decision to move the German Parliament from Bonn back to its pre-war home in Berlin. In other cities, there is concern that businesses will relocate to a new Berlin. Hamburg, for example, the focus of Germany's rapidly growing media industry, is particularly worried as it is only two and a half hours down the motorway from Berlin.

Already, IBM have moved their headquarters to Berlin, and it is rumoured that Mercedes-Benz may do the same.

EC Regional Policy Statement, 1993 (adapted)

Source C Rebuilding Berlin: costs and benefits

Examine all the evidence shown on these two pages.

1 The chart below states two key points shown by Source A. Draw similar charts for Sources B, C, D and E, and suggest two key points for each.

Source	Key points
A	Berlin is the capital of Germany. A border used to divide East and West Berlin.

2 It has been suggested that the rebuilding of Berlin will damage other parts of Germany. Do you agree? Explain why.

3 Produce a publicity brochure designed to attract new business into Berlin. Your brochure should include graphical and written information.

4 Draw a map to show population change in Berlin compared to the rest of Germany. You will have to decide on the best way of showing this information.

5 Imagine that you are a councillor in Hamburg. Write a letter to the Government explaining why you oppose the rebuilding of Berlin.

6 *The Chancellor of Germany has asked you to advise on the costs and benefits of making Berlin the capital once more. Use all the evidence that you have collected and constructed to produce the report.*

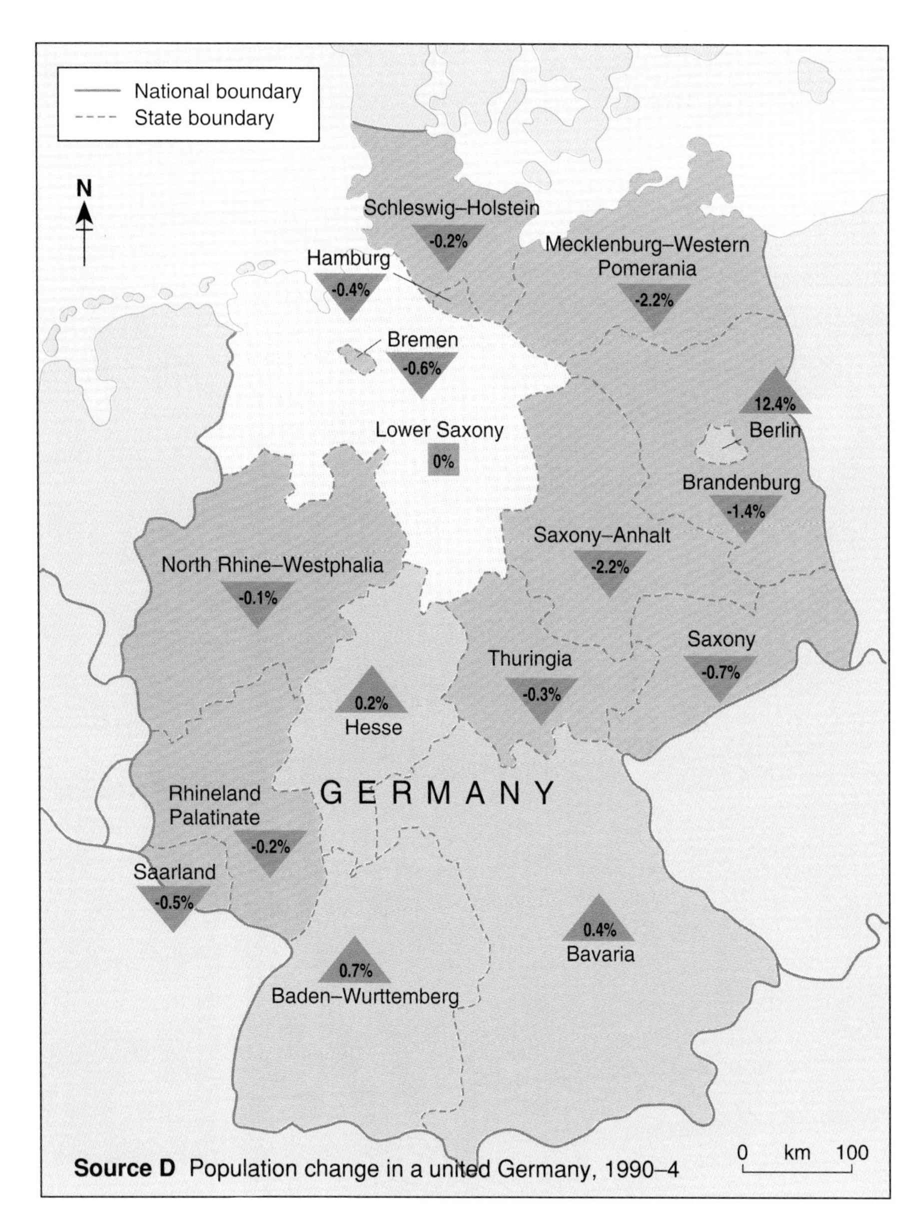

Source D Population change in a united Germany, 1990–4

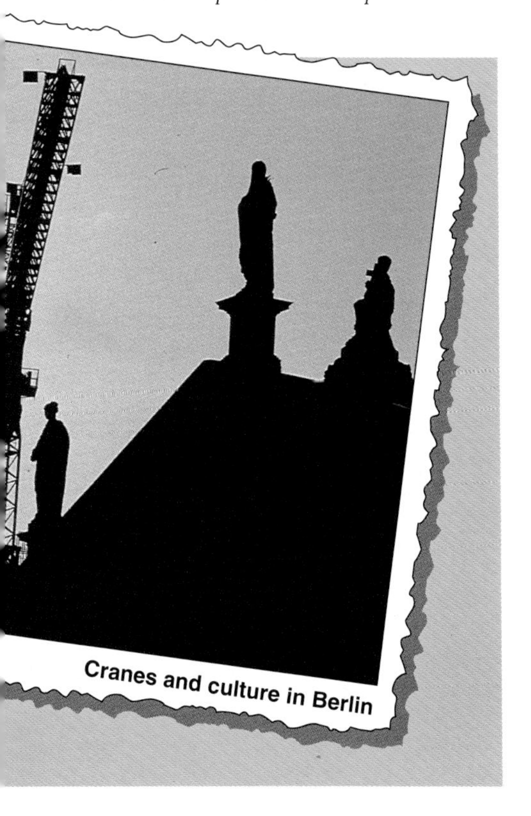
Cranes and culture in Berlin

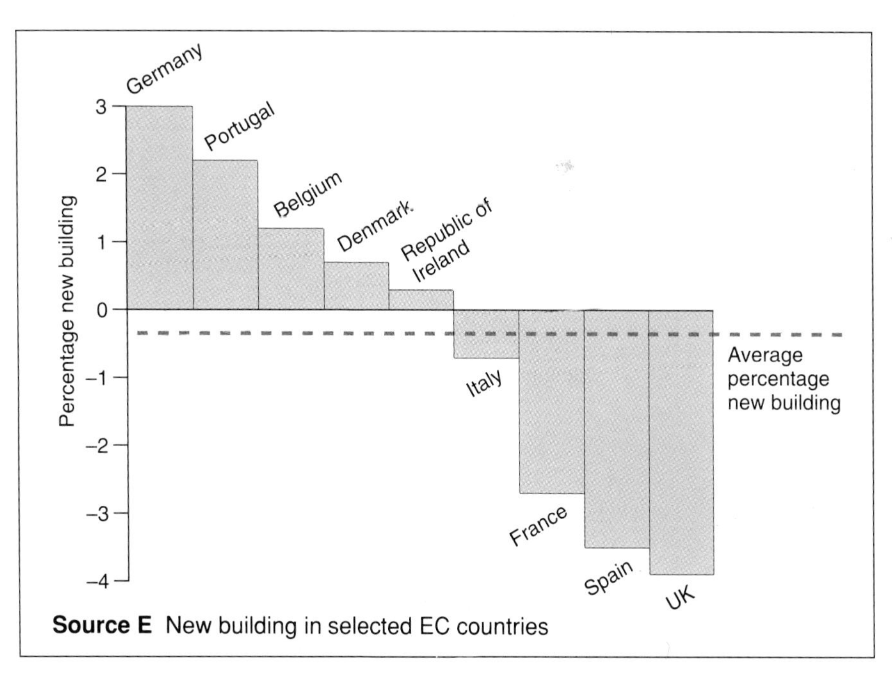

Source E New building in selected EC countries

3·3 'Guestworkers' in Germany

Racist violence sweeps Germany

Turkish demonstrator stirs memories of German racism

Police and firefighters examine a gutted building in Mölln where three Turks were killed

Mölln is a small town 50 kilometres from Hamburg. 'Guestworkers' have lived there for more than 20 years. In the year to November 1992 there were 16 violent deaths. In one incident, two Turkish girls, aged 10 and 14, and a 51-year-old woman were killed when youths attacked their home. Nine other people were injured including an 82-year-old woman and a baby.

Source A Tension soars after death fires, November 1992

Reunification has led to population movement within Germany. It has also affected the patterns of migration from other countries. Migrant workers have been moving to Germany since the early 1950s. Most were temporary workers from Turkey, hired to do the poorly paid jobs. After working for some time, many 'GUESTWORKERS' wanted to make Germany their home. In 1990, 5.4 per cent of the population were immigrants, many of whom were 'guestworkers'.

There was a rapid increase in racist attacks against migrant workers throughout Germany in 1992. At the same time, the number of neo-Nazi groups, who are against immigration, grew.

1 Study Source A.
a Describe the two scenes.
b List words which summarise your feelings about the scenes shown.
c Imagine that you are a Turkish 'guestworker' living in Mölln. Write a letter to your family in Turkey. Tell them that you are safe. Describe what has happened and how you feel about it.

2 **a** Why do you think there are so many 'guestworkers' in Germany?
b Suggest reasons to explain why few wish to return home.

3 **a** In pairs, discuss and list the possible causes of racist violence. Share your views with the class.
b 'Racism is the result of ignorance and fear. It should be dealt with swiftly and firmly.' What are your views about this statement?
c What do you think the German authorities should do to prevent further racist violence?
d Does your answer to part **c** conflict with any of your earlier views? Explain your answer.

Patterns of migration

Since the Second World War the number of migrants to Germany has steadily increased. Germany's constitution allowed foreigners to settle temporarily in the country. In 1973 the EC Parliament was concerned about the number of migrants entering Europe and imposed strict limits. People thought that many 'guestworkers' would return home. By this time, however, many had brought their families to Germany. Some had young children who regarded themselves as German citizens.

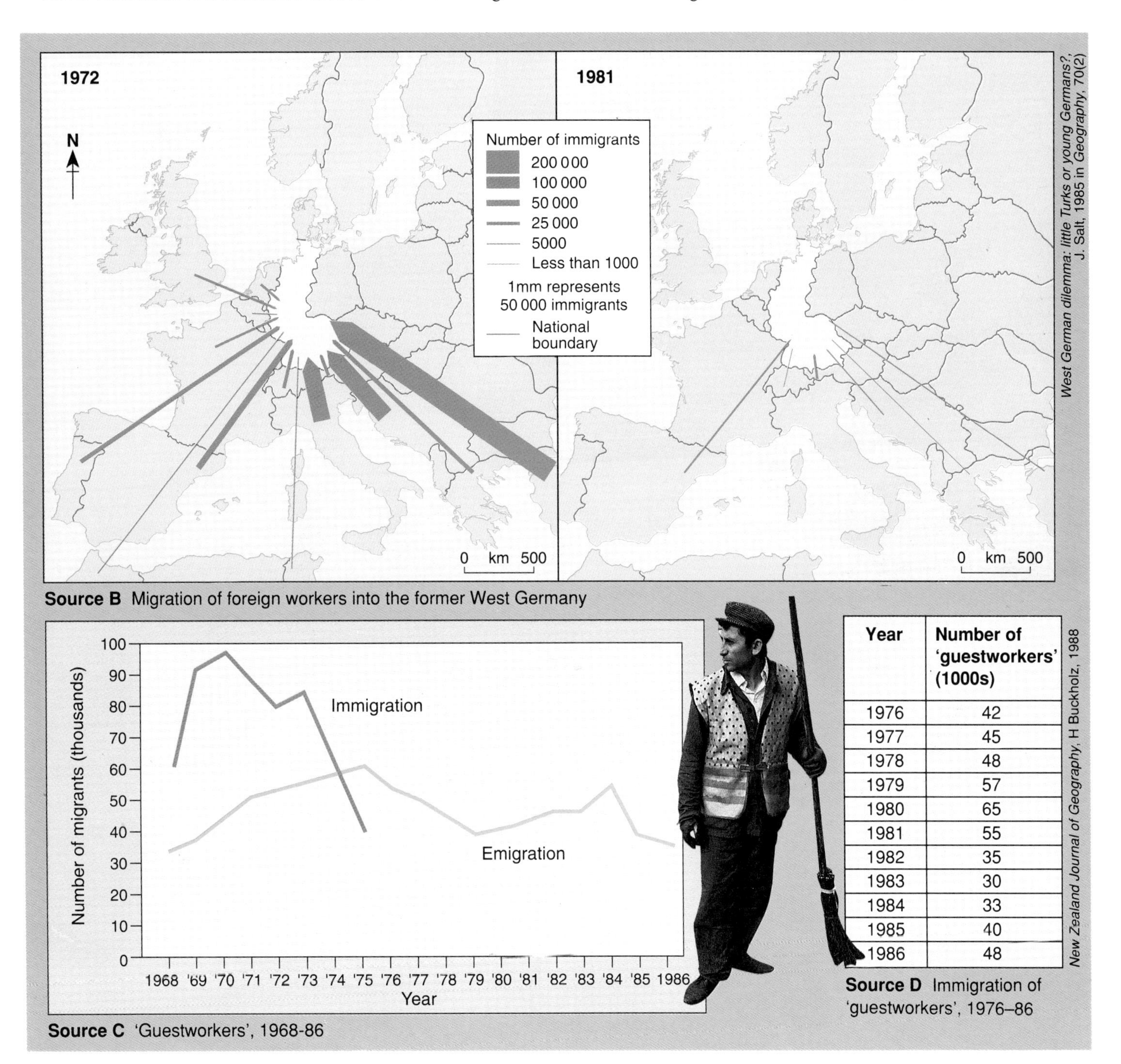

Source B Migration of foreign workers into the former West Germany

Source C 'Guestworkers', 1968-86

Year	Number of 'guestworkers' (1000s)
1976	42
1977	45
1978	48
1979	57
1980	65
1981	55
1982	35
1983	30
1984	33
1985	40
1986	48

Source D Immigration of 'guestworkers', 1976–86

4 Using Source B and an atlas:
a On an outline map of Europe name the countries from which people migrated to West Germany in 1972. For each country, state the number of migrants involved.
b Describe the pattern of migration into West Germany in 1972. What surprises you about this pattern? Suggest reasons to explain the pattern.
c What effect did EC legislation have on patterns of migration in 1981?

5 Study Sources C and D.
a Make a copy of Source C and, using Source D, complete the line graph to show immigration of 'guest-workers' up to 1986.
b Draw a line across your completed graph at the 1973 level of immigration.
c What do you notice about immigration before and after 1973?
d How does the pattern of EMIGRATION *compare with the pattern of immigration?*

3·4 'Guestworkers' and employment

Although 'guestworkers' do many of Germany's low-paid but essential jobs, they have no rights of citizenship. Their temporary status has led to an uncertainty over their right to live in Germany and their employment. It has also led to a lack of investment in their general welfare and living conditions.

Source A Turkish 'guestworkers' in Frankfurt

Job	'Guestworker' employment (%)
Construction industry	9
Car manufacture	7.8
Electrical goods manufacture	7.8
Retail/wholesale trades	6.4
Machinery manufacture	5.4
Hotel and restaurant trades	4.5
Others (e.g. public service workers, such as cleaners, refuse collectors, gardeners)	59.1

New Zealand Journal of Geography, H Buckholz, 1988

Source B The jobs that 'guestworkers' do

City	'Guestworkers' (% city population)
Berlin	14
Duisburg	13
Dusseldorf	16
Frankfurt	25
Cologne	15
Mannheim	16
Munich	17
Nuremberg	13
Stuttgart	18

Datenreport, H Buckholz, 1987

Source C Cities with a high number of 'guestworkers'

1 Study Source A. Describe the type of job being carried out by the Turkish 'guestworkers'.

2 Study Source B.
a Draw a divided bar chart to show the jobs of 'guestworkers'.
b What type of jobs are not included under 'guestworker' employment?
c Suggest reasons to explain why 'guestworkers' are employed in the jobs shown in your chart.

3 Study Source C.
a On a large copy of the map, use a suitable technique to show the percentage of 'guestworkers' in each city.
b Which parts of Germany appear not to have large concentrations of 'guestworkers'?
c Suggest a reason to explain this.

Scapegoats for unemployment?

Year	'Guestworkers' (% total population)	Unemployment (% total population)
1970	4.3	0.5
1974	6.7	1.5
1978	6.5	2.5
1982	7.6	6.9
1986	7.4	8.1
1990	8.2	5.1

Source D Germany: 'guestworkers' and unemployment

Jobless growth fuels German gloom

Unemployment in West Germany rose drastically last month to more than 2 million ... The rise brought the unemployment rate to 7.4 per cent ... the number of West Germans on short-time working rose by 171,000 to 649,600 in December ... industrial orders in October and November last year were 9.4 per cent down on a year before, while industrial output fell by almost 5 per cent in the same period.

David Gow, *The Guardian*, 8 January 1993

Source E Germany: rising unemployment

Source F A Turkish spokesperson

The Turkish community demand better protection for the 1.74 million Turks living in Germany. We are concerned that if nothing is done, young Turks will arm themselves and take the law into their own hands. Young Turks are particularly angry because, although many were born in Germany, they have been denied citizenship. To be a German it is essential to have at least one parent born here.

German riots go on after Turks die in firebombing

Flowers and a dozen teddy bears lay in front of the charred remains of the two-storey house where two women and three girls, aged four, nine and thirteen, died. At the same time rioting Turkish workers smashed windows and cars in Solingen, 80km north of Bonn. Motorways were blocked and the road to the airport was closed for several hours. Dozens of people were injured and 17 were arrested.

Source G Turks riot in Solingen, 31 May 1993

4 Study Source D.
a On the same axes draw two line graphs to show how the percentage of 'guestworkers' and unemployment in Germany have changed between 1970 and 1990. Clearly label your graphs.
b In 1993 'guestworkers' made up 5.4 per cent of Germany's population and unemployment was at 7.4 per cent. Extend your graph to show this information.
c Predict what the figures will be in the year 2000.
d Describe any relationship that appears to exist between the percentage of 'guestworkers' and the percentage of unemployment.
e Why might it be dangerous to make such comparisons?
f How does the information in Source E help to explain the changes in the percentage of unemployment?

5 Study Sources F and G.
a With a partner discuss your views on:
- violence against 'guestworkers' and their families
- the reaction of young Turks to violence against 'guestworkers'.

b Imagine that you are the editor of a national newspaper. Write an editorial of no more than 250 words, summarising the outcomes of your discussion.

4·1 NIGERIA: PEOPLE AND THE LAND

Nigeria is Africa's most populated country. Some of its people are migrating from areas where they have traditionally lived. Why is this happening? Which areas are most affected? What are the impacts of these changes?

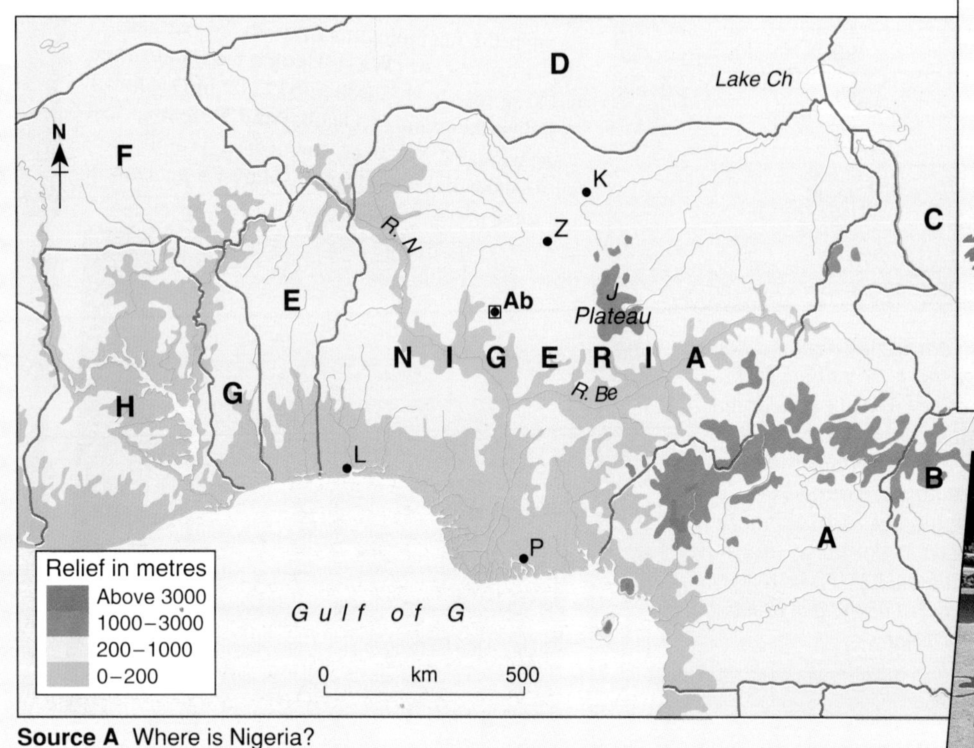

Source A Where is Nigeria?

N

The British Isles on the same scale as Nigeria
Total area = 314 771km²

Number enrolled in primary school (% age group): 98 (1983), 70 (1989)
Number enrolled in higher education (% age group): 2 (1983), 3 (1990)

1 On a large copy of Source A and with the help of an atlas, mark and name the following:
- countries A–H,
- rivers Be and N,
- Lake Ch,
- Gulf of G,
- cities Ab, K, L, P and Z,
- J Plateau.

2 **a** Use Source A to measure (in km) the distances across Nigeria from:
- north to south,
- west to east.

b Use your answers to estimate the area of Nigeria.
c Use Source B and your answer to **b** to calculate the POPULATION DENSITY (the number of people per km²) of Nigeria in the 1980s and the 1990s.
d How much bigger is Nigeria than the British Isles?

3 Work in a small group and study Source B. The purpose of the group is to advise the World Health Organisation on the social development of Nigeria. Write a short report to explain changes in the social conditions between 1980 and 1990. Your report should be written under the following headings:
- Population size and structure
- People and the economy
- Population and employment
- Health care and education
- Summary of social changes.

Illustrate your report with appropriate maps, tables, graphs and diagrams.

	1984	1990
Estimated population (millions)	96.5	115.5
Estimated urban population (% total population)	30	35
Estimated employment (% total population)		
Agriculture	68	45
Industry	12	4
Services	20	51
GNP per capita ($US)	730	290
National debt (billion $US)	11.8	33.7
Daily calorie supply (kcal)	2022	2312

World Bank Development Reports, 1986 and 1992 and *Human Development Report*, UNDP, 1992

Source B Population and social development, Nigeria

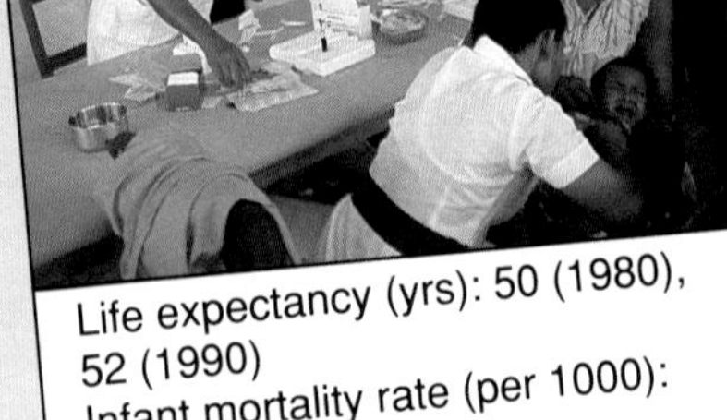

Life expectancy (yrs): 50 (1980), 52 (1990)
Infant mortality rate (per 1000): 110 (1984), 98 (1990)

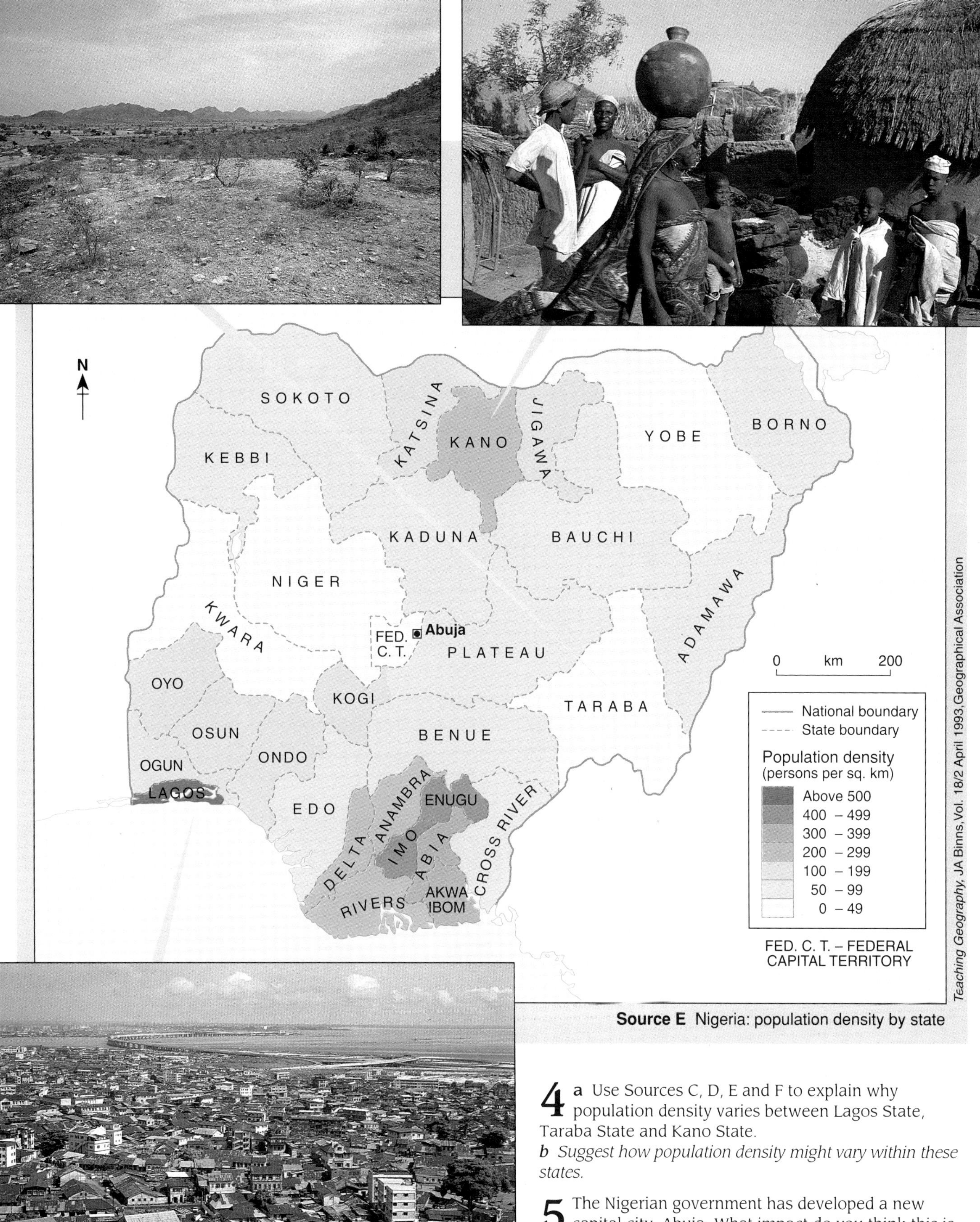

Source C Taraba State: poor upland soils

Source D Kano State: village life

Source E Nigeria: population density by state

Source F Lagos State: a housing estate

4 **a** Use Sources C, D, E and F to explain why population density varies between Lagos State, Taraba State and Kano State.

b *Suggest how population density might vary within these states.*

5 The Nigerian government has developed a new capital city, Abuja. What impact do you think this is having on:

- the population density of the Federal Capital Territory
- the people in the surrounding states
- the old capital city of Lagos?

4·2 Land reform . . .

Nigeria is an economically developing country. As part of its development programme, the Nigerian government introduced land reforms to modernise agriculture.

Farming in Kachia

For hundreds of generations the Gwari and Jaba tribes have farmed the plateau region of central Nigeria, an area abandoned during slave-trading times. The 1978 Land Use Act ordered all farmers to prove ownership of their land. Most were unable to do so because they held no documents. As a result, the Government took possession of their land.

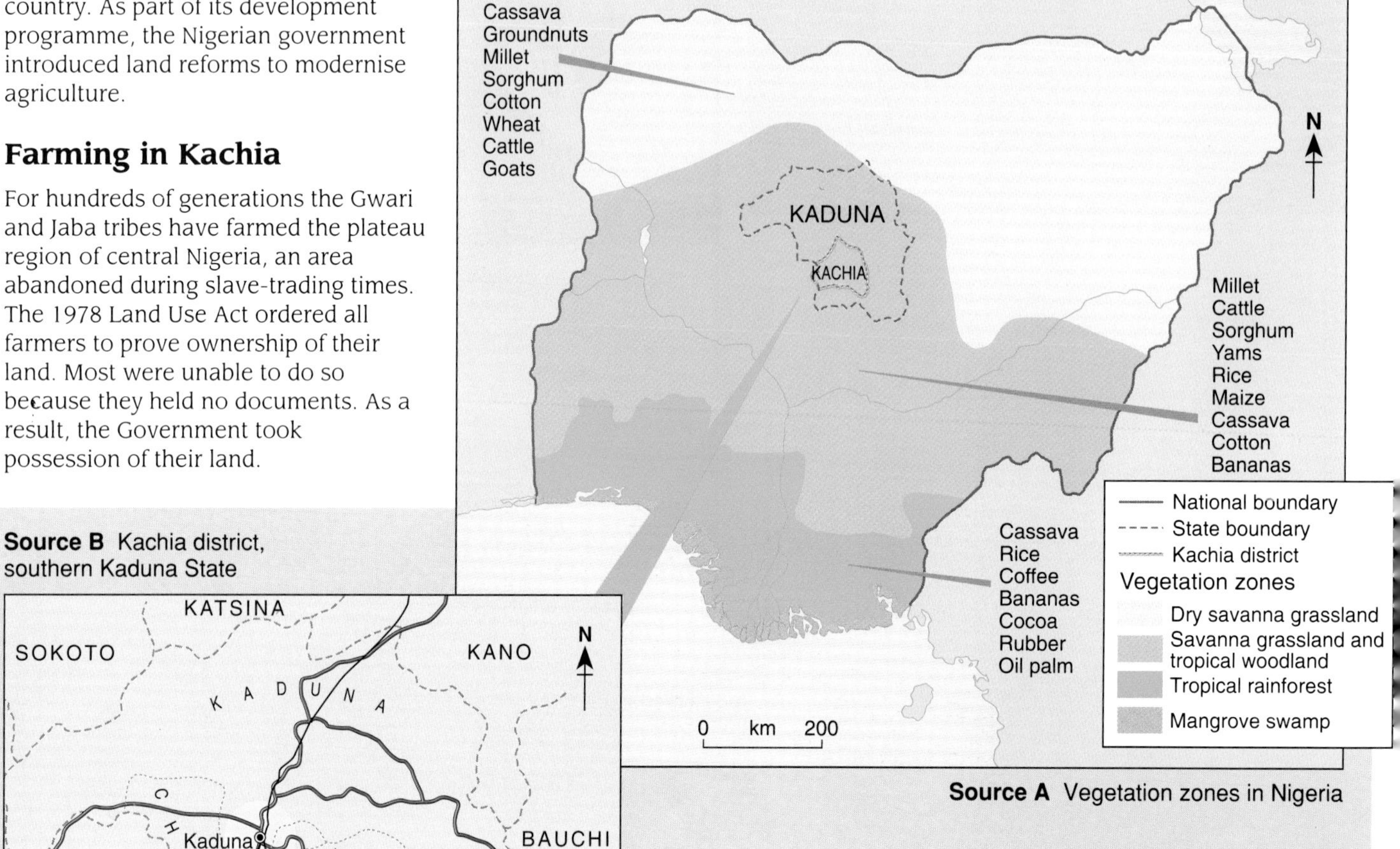

Source A Vegetation zones in Nigeria

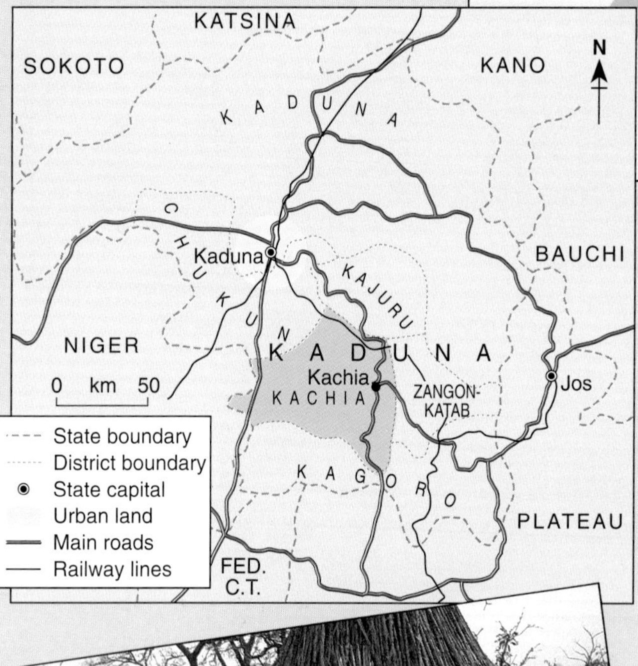

Source B Kachia district, southern Kaduna State

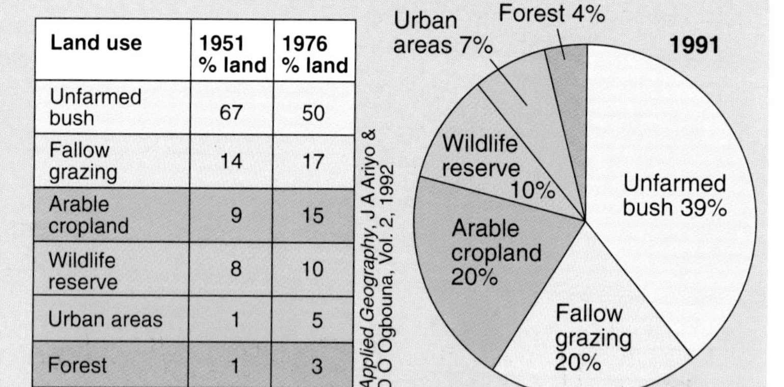

Land use	1951 % land	1976 % land
Unfarmed bush	67	50
Fallow grazing	14	17
Arable cropland	9	15
Wildlife reserve	8	10
Urban areas	1	5
Forest	1	3

Source C Changing land use in Nigeria

Source D Members of the Gwari tribe collecting yams

1 a Describe the patterns of vegetation shown in Source A.
b Draw a sketch map to help you describe the location of Kachia district.

2 Study Source C.
a Draw two pie charts to show the land use in Nigeria in 1951 and 1976.
b Use Source C and your pie charts to describe how land use has changed since 1951.
c Which of the land use types would you expect to find in Kachia district? Explain your answer.

... or destroying a way of life?

In our village land belongs to the whole community. Everyone works together to get the best out of the land. Growing good crops is difficult because of the dry and dusty soils.

Source E Traditional maize farming in Nigeria

The land is cleared

The land is fertilised with manure and ashes

The land is hoed and seed sown

A crop of maize

The crop is harvested

The harvest is winnowed to loosen the grain

Harvested land is cleared. A new crop is planted or the land left fallow for 8–10 years

3 Study Source E. Draw a diagram to explain the traditional farming system.

4 Study Source F. Comment on the importance of agriculture to people living in the Kachia district.

5 The United Nations (UN) has received several thousand complaints about the changes resulting from land reform. You have been asked to investigate.
a In a small group, brainstorm and list the key questions that you should ask.
b Design a plan for investigating the complaints. In your plan, identify the people that you would want to question.
c Explain briefly to whom and how you will report your findings.

6 *Produce a briefing paper for the UN investigating team. It should provide details of Kachia under the following headings:*

- *Where it is*
- *What it is like*
- *Farming practices*
- *Patterns of land ownership and trading*
- *How the area is changing.*

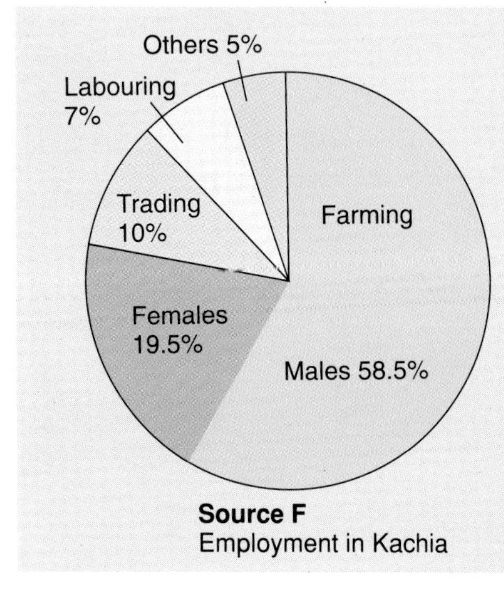

Source F Employment in Kachia

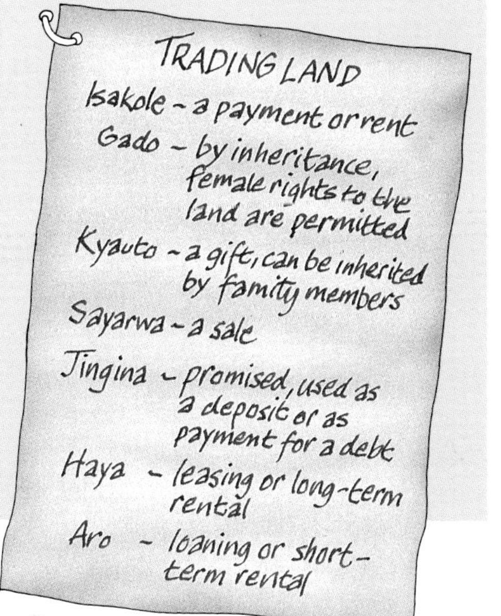
TRADING LAND

Isakole – a payment or rent

Gado – by inheritance, female rights to the land are permitted

Kyauto – a gift, can be inherited by family members

Sayarwa – a sale

Jingina – promised, used as a deposit or as payment for a debt

Haya – leasing or long-term rental

Aro – loaning or short-term rental

Source G Traditional methods of trading land

4·3 The costs of land reform

Land was taken from the farmers who could not prove ownership. They received no compensation. Farmers who held documents had their land bought by the Government. Compensation was paid for their crops, trees and buildings.

Many farmers regarded compensation as unfair and damaging to their tribal status. Over 65 per cent were unhappy with the payments they received. Some richer farmers are trying to get a better deal by appealing to Nigeria's High Court.

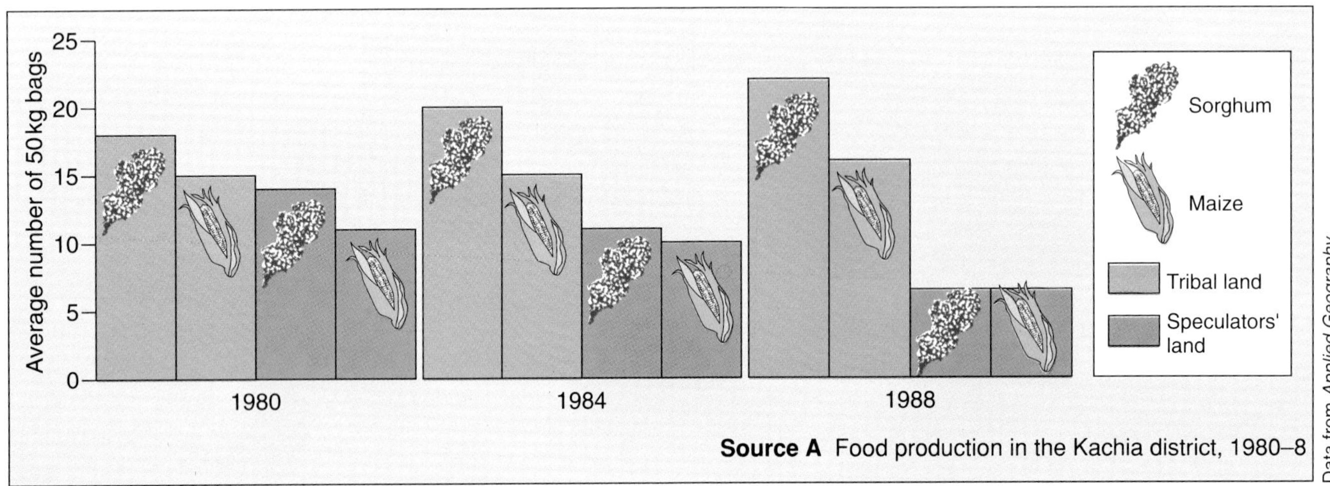

Source A Food production in the Kachia district, 1980–8

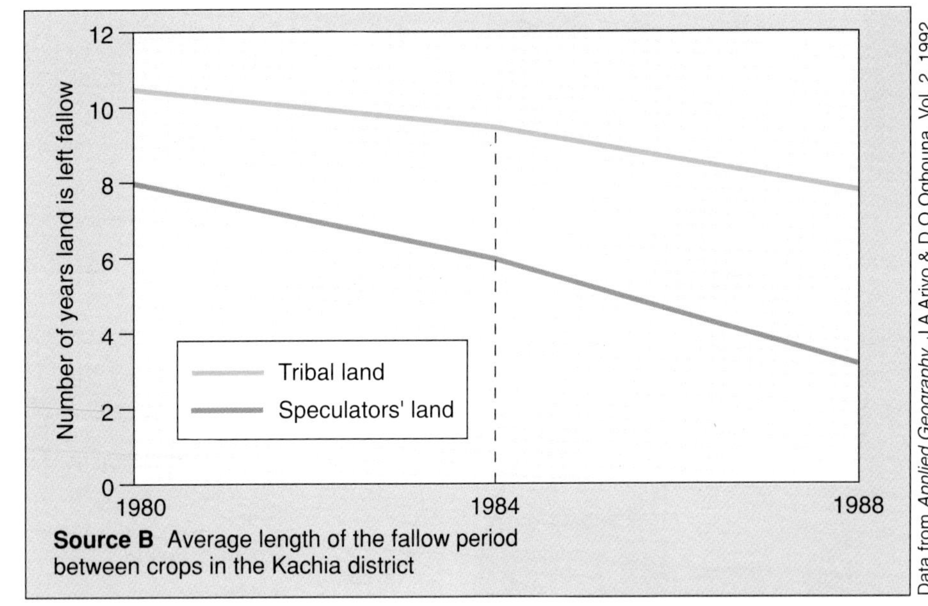

Source B Average length of the fallow period between crops in the Kachia district

Data from *Applied Geography*, J A Ariyo & D O Ogbouna, Vol. 2, 1992

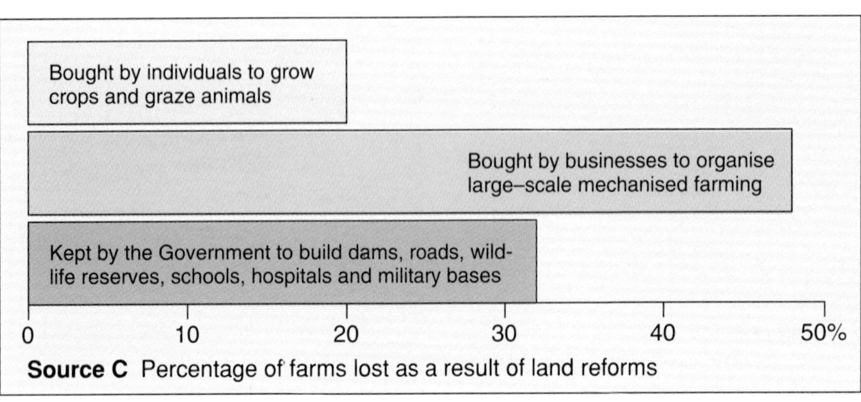

Source C Percentage of farms lost as a result of land reforms

Data from *Applied Geography*, J A Ariyo & D O Ogbouna, Vol. 2, 1992

What happened to the land?

As a result of land reforms, large companies and wealthy individuals bought vast areas of land from the Government. They did so because they expected land values to increase. These people are called LAND SPECULATORS.

1 **a** How did the 1978 Land Use Act affect farm ownership in Kachia district?
b Suggest reasons which might explain why this Act was passed.
c Briefly explain what is meant by the term 'land speculation'.

2 **a** What does Source A show about food production on tribal lands and on land owned by speculators?
b How does Source B help to explain your answer?
c What surprises you about the evidence that you have found? Explain your answer.
d How might farmers increase crop production without increasing the length of the fallow period?

3 **a** Why were so many farmers unhappy with the amount of compensation they received?
b What are your feelings about the arrangements for compensation?

Source D To which places did the farmers migrate?

Kano
N
Zaria
Kaduna
Kachia
Jos
Other cities
1mm width is 10% of migrants
Road
Railway
0 km 50

The impact on farmers

Speculators allowed farmers to rent small areas of land. These farmers tried to maintain their incomes. Many reduced the number of fallow years between crops to increase harvests. However, they realised that they would not be able to survive in the long term. Eventually, the land reforms forced many of these farmers to abandon their homes, villages and traditional ways of life. Estimates suggest that as many as 15 000 people may have been affected throughout Kaduna State.

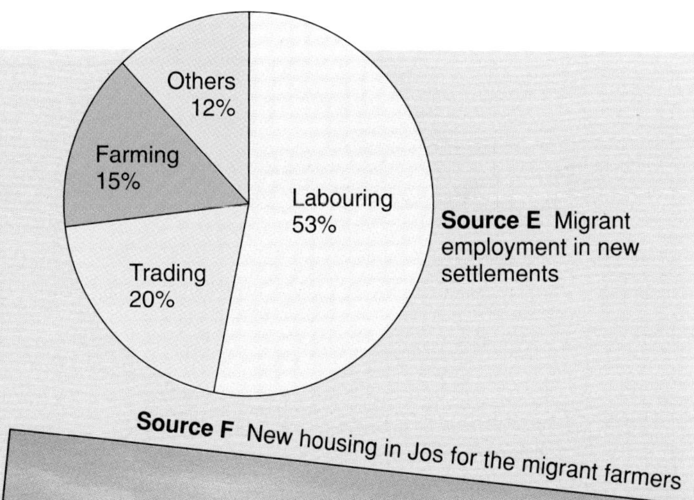

Source E Migrant employment in new settlements

Source F New housing in Jos for the migrant farmers

Source G Report from Bayero University, Kano

It is extremely doubtful that the reforms will organize land for the common good of all Nigerians. Land reforms separate people's homes from their place of work, increase industrial development and the exploitation of cheap labour. Farmers work for a wage and rent their homes, while the wealthy benefit from schools, universities and hospitals.

4 **a** Calculate the percentage of MIGRANTS moving to the four cities in Source D.
b Measure the distances from Kachia to each of the cities.
c How does your answer to part **b** help to explain your answer to part **a**?
d Suggest other reasons to explain the patterns of migration of farmers.

5 Study Source E. How does the employment structure for migrants in the cities differ from that of the people still living in Kachia? (Look back at Source F, page 25.)

6 Imagine that you are a migrant worker living in one of the houses shown in Source F. Write a letter home comparing your living conditions with those you left in Kachia.

7 Study Source G.
a What are your views on the report produced by Bayero University?
b How do you think the Nigerian government should respond to this report?

5·1 TRANSPORT AND TRAVEL

Transport within and between countries is essential for economic development. Different types of transport have advantages and disadvantages. How do transport networks change and grow? How important is international travel for development?

Types of transport

Source A On the move

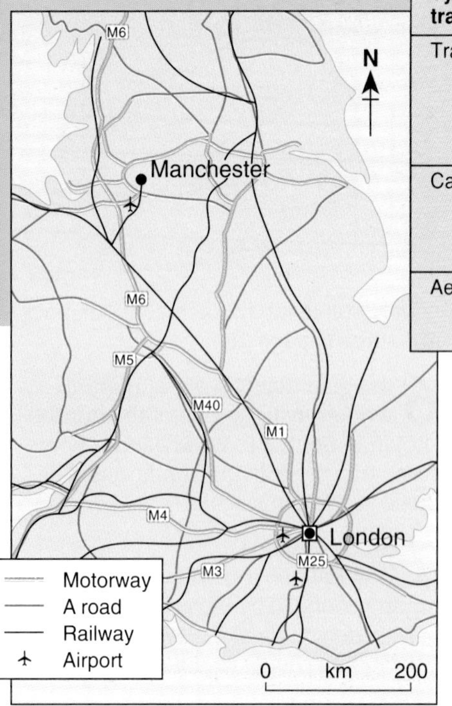

Type of transport	Time taken	Cost in 1993	Convenience
Train	2 hours 40 minutes (direct)	Per person: up to £41 one way, £32 day return (prices depend on time and day of travel).	Seventeen direct trains each weekday to Euston. Tube or bus to central London.
Car	About 3–4 hours depending on traffic	About £13 one way for petrol, plus cost of using car e.g. tax and insurance.	Leave any time, door to door.
Aeroplane	1 hour	Per person: £69 one way £92 return.	Eleven flights each weekday to Heathrow, five to Gatwick. Tube or bus, or train, tube or bus to central London.

Source B Manchester to London – how to travel?

1 Work in pairs. Study Source A.
a List the different types of transport.
b Rearrange your list, putting the types of transport in the order in which you think they were developed. Explain how you decided on your order.
c Which do you think is the most expensive form of transport? Why is this so?

2 Study Sources A and B and work out the best type of transport for a journey from Manchester to London for:
a a group of three adults going for the weekend.
b a business executive going to an important meeting for the day.
c a student going to college.
Discuss the advantages and disadvantages of each choice.

Moving goods

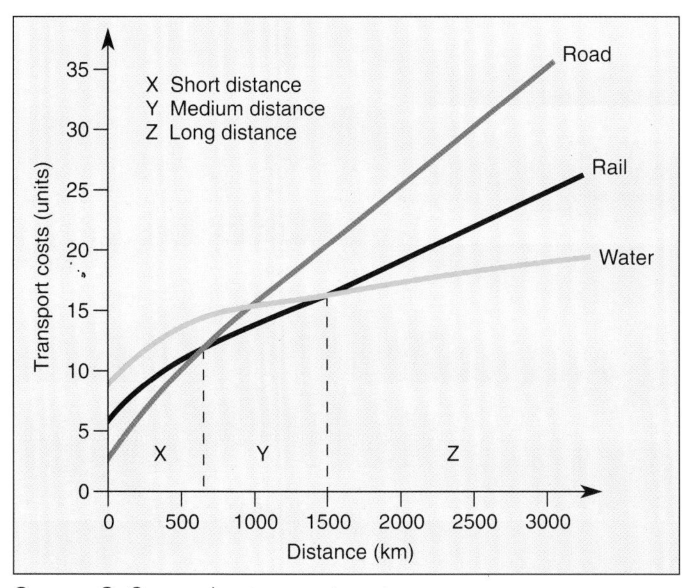

Source C Comparing transport costs

	Nigeria	UK
Area	923 770 km²	244 880 km²
Population	109 170 000	57 400 000
GNP per person	$250	$16 100

Source D Country profiles, 1989

	Nigeria	UK
Private cars	400 000	20 925 000
Taxis, buses, vans, lorries	50 000	2 684 700
Passengers carried:		
domestic flights	638 000	16 075 000
international flights	211 000	30 279 000

Source E Passenger and freight transport, 1989

Transport and economic development

Source F Travelling by road in Nigeria: 'bush taxis' are quick and comfortable and there are regular bus services

3 Study Source C.
a What is the cheapest type of transport for moving goods:
• 500 km, • 1000 km, • 2000 km?
b Draw a line graph to show that air freight is: • three times more expensive than road at 250 km, • four times more expensive than rail at 500 km, • five times more expensive than water transport at 3000 km and over.
c Working in small groups, discuss which types of transport you might use to move the following: coal, letters, diamonds, milk, dishwashers.
d Use your list to help you explain those factors, other than cost, that might influence your choice.

4 Using Source D, write three sentences comparing Nigeria with the UK.

5 Using Sources D, E, F and G, compare the MOBILITY of road and air passengers in Nigeria and the UK.

6 *Using all the sources on these pages, write a sentence to describe a possible relationship between transport and ECONOMIC DEVELOPMENT.*

Source G Jos airport: Nigeria Airways and other private companies operate domestic flights

Trade routes in West Africa

Before AD 1000, the major trade routes in West Africa crossed the Sahara Desert. Empires and major cities developed in the Sahel at the end of the trans-Saharan routes. Traders bought and sold horses, cattle, millet, gold and slaves.

European traders arrived from about 1470 onwards. They bought gold and slaves in exchange for salt, then for guns and cloth. Later, trade grew in products such as timber, beeswax, ivory, hides and palm oil. European trade routes used sea transport.

By 1900, British trading companies were very powerful in Nigeria. They EXPORTED goods such as groundnuts and tin. The British government set up protectorates, and in 1914 Nigeria became a British colony until its independence in 1960.

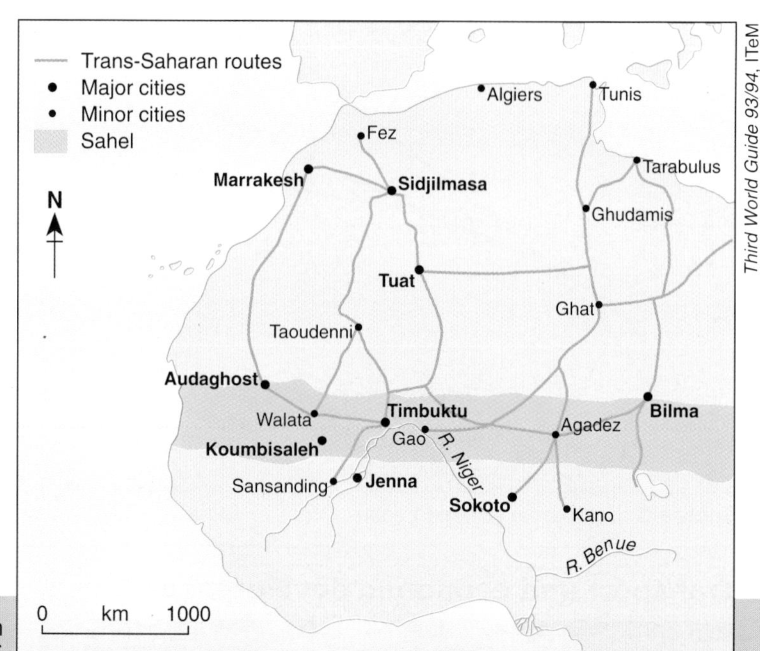

Source A West African trade routes 1000–1775

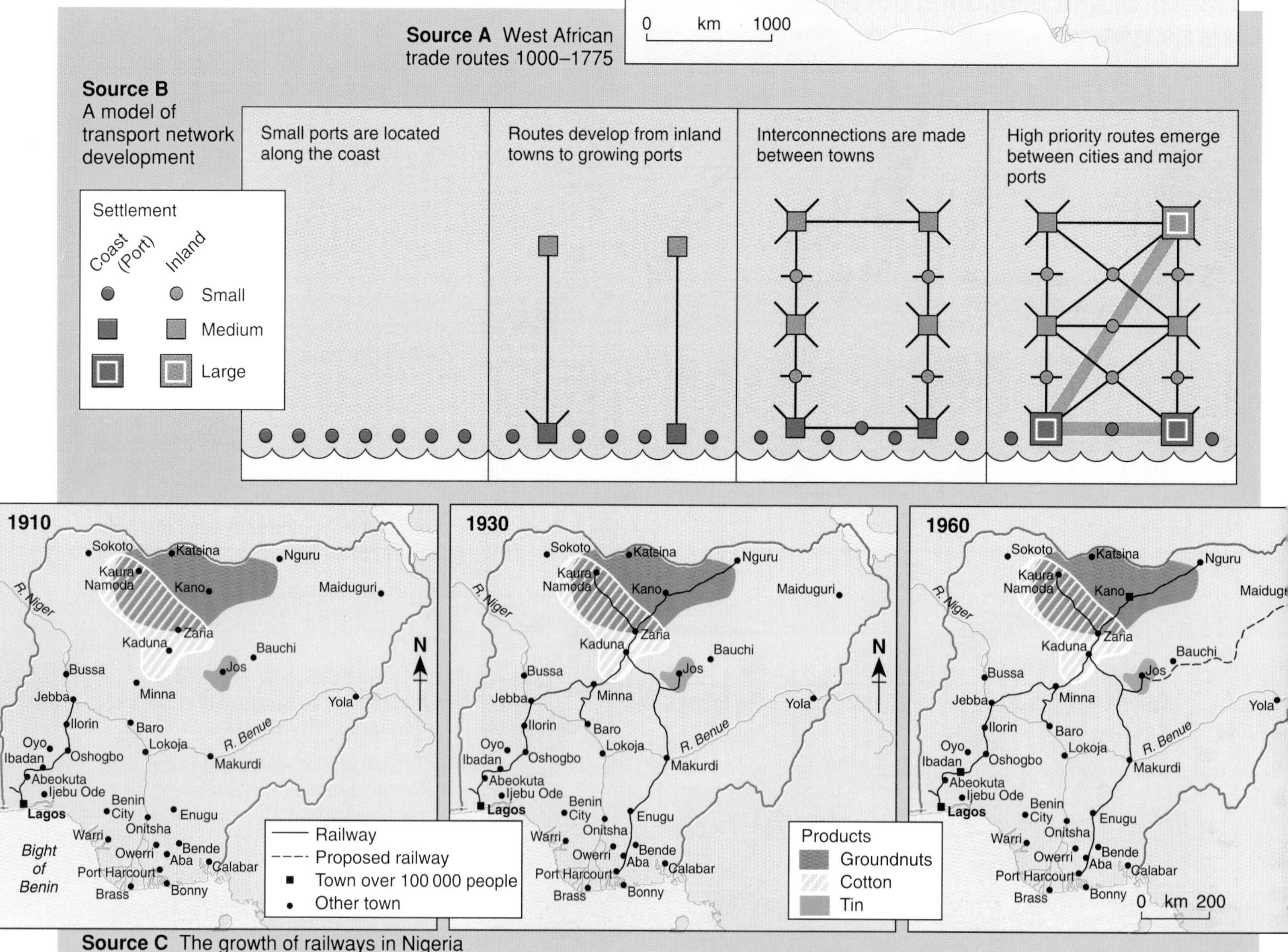

Source C The growth of railways in Nigeria

1 Study Source B. According to this model, what are the four stages of growth in the development of a transport network?

2 Compare Source B with Source A. How far does the model fit the development of trade routes before 1775?

3 Compare Source B with Source C. How far does the model fit the development of the railway network?

4 Study Source C.
a Using evidence from Source B, explain why railways extended into northern Nigeria.
b What was the effect of the railway network on the exploitation of Nigeria? Explain your answer.

5 In a small group, discuss:
a the effect of colonialism on transport networks.
b the definition of economic development suggested by Source B.

After independence

After Nigeria became independent, its government chose to expand the road network rather than the railways. The rail line between Jos and Maiduguri (Source C) was completed, but the network as a whole was allowed to run down. Nigeria now has about 115 000 km of roads, half of them surfaced. The main roads are superb, and road transport is fast – except in the rainy season. However, it is expensive and difficult to maintain all-weather roads in a tropical climate.

Source D This rural settlement in Ondo State is accessible only by a road which gets flooded during the wet season. A tarmac road would greatly improve the villagers' QUALITY OF LIFE

Source E Loading groundnuts on to lorries in Kano, northern Nigeria

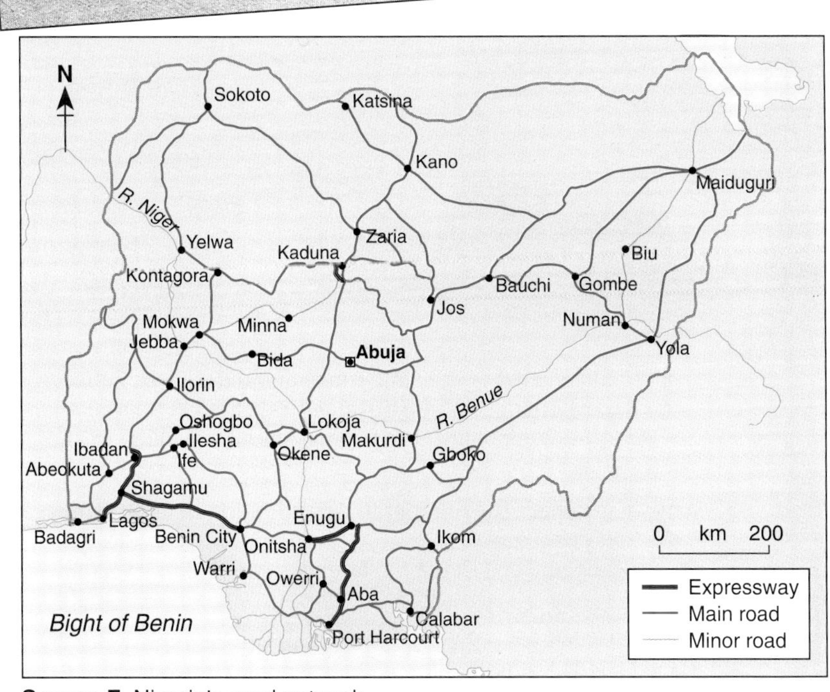

Source F Nigeria's road network

6 Suggest reasons why the Nigerian government chose to spend money on roads rather than railways. Consider:
- ACCESSIBILITY in the countryside (Source D)
- Nigeria produces and refines oil; its petrol prices are about the lowest in the world
- your answers to **3** and **6** on page 29.

7 **a** Use Source F to plan a route for moving the groundnuts in Source E to the port of Lagos.
b Measure the distance each lorry will travel.
c Use Source C on page 29 to estimate the cost in units of each trip.
d Compare this cost with the cost in units of using rail transport over the same distance.
e Do you think the Nigerian government was right to expand the road network? Give reasons for your views.

8 *Make a list of the factors that Nigerian PLANNERS should consider for the next stage in expanding their transport networks.*

Nigeria and the UK

I travel to Nigeria on business from time to time. I am not altogether impressed by Nigeria Airways. Domestic flights are cheap, but they are unreliable and you may have to wait ages. There may be one or two flights a day or only two a week. I always have to arrive very early to be sure of a seat – you can't reserve one in advance.

I prefer Kano airport to Lagos and I try to use it whenever I can. None of the airports have rail links, so I have to take local taxis when I arrive. You need lots of patience and a sense of humour for travelling by air in Nigeria!

Prodeepta Das, photographer

I fly frequently within the UK and sometimes abroad. There are air shuttle services between the UK's largest cities – it's pretty good: you can turn up half an hour before the flight, and off you go! If the plane is full, you wait about an hour for the next one. Sometimes, however, there are long delays because of problems with the air traffic control system.

On international flights I must reserve a seat. Getting to and from the airport isn't usually a problem: many cities have special links by rail or airport buses, or I can take a taxi. Traffic jams on the roads can be frustrating!

Flights aren't cheap, and if I have time I sometimes take the train. Travelling is a chore, so I want it to be as efficient as possible.

Kate Harris, Publishing Director

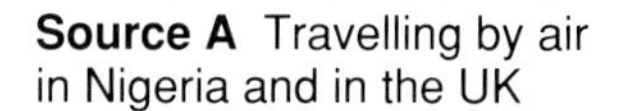

Source A Travelling by air in Nigeria and in the UK

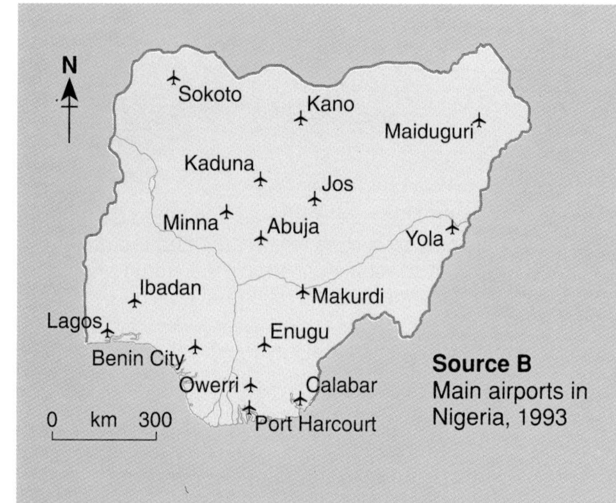

Source B Main airports in Nigeria, 1993

Distances in Nigeria are so great that domestic air travel is popular. It takes 48 hours from Lagos to Maiduguri by train, compared with two and a half hours by air. In the UK, on the other hand, most airline traffic is international. The UK, like other wealthy countries, has a well-developed INFRASTRUCTURE of airports and airport services.

Source C Main airports in the UK, 1993

Source D Passenger traffic at main UK airports, 1984–93

Airport	Terminating passengers (millions)		Percentage change
	1984	1993	1984–93
London Heathrow	29.2	45.9	57.2
London Gatwick	14.0	19.8	41.4
Manchester	5.93	12.5	111
Glasgow	2.75	4.80	74.5
Birmingham	1.67	3.88	132
London Luton	1.80	1.91	6.11
Edinburgh	1.49	2.59	73.8
Belfast (International)	1.58	2.25	42.4
Aberdeen	1.76	2.19	24.4
Newcastle	1.07	2.00	86.9
East Midlands	1.08	1.28	18.5
London Stansted	0.53	2.40	353
Leeds–Bradford	0.40	0.70	75
Bristol	0.42	1.12	167
Cardiff	0.43	0.75	74.4
Belfast (City)	0.18	0.61	239
Teesside	0.28	0.35	25
Liverpool	0.23	0.47	104

Civil Aviation Authority, 1993 and the airports, 1993

1 a Make a list of the similarities and differences between the experiences of the business travellers in Source A.
b Describe Prodeepta Das's feelings about travelling to and in Nigeria.

2 a Compare the number and distribution of airports in Sources B and C.
b Suggest reasons for any differences you find.

3 Study Source D.
a Which were the busiest five airports in 1993?
b Which five airports had the biggest percentage increase in passenger traffic between 1984 and 1993?

Manchester airport

Manchester is a HUB for domestic passengers travelling to and from the North-West, but most of its passenger traffic is on international flights. Manchester has worked hard to develop as an international airport, especially for flights to the USA and Europe. Cities like Manchester and Birmingham have good road and rail links for onward travel. They also have international facilities such as hotels, conference halls and exhibition centres.

4 Read what Kate Harris says in Source A, and study Sources E and F. Make a list of what travellers expect from a good airport.

5 Study Sources C and D.
a Name the airports that compete with Manchester and Birmingham for business. How much less passenger traffic do they get?
b On Source C, find another pair of airports that are competing for business. For one of these airports, write a letter to the city and airport authorities, advising them what they should do to win customers.

Flying from Manchester

- Last year 12.5 million people passed through Manchester airport.
- Seventy-six airlines and over 200 tour operators operate from the airport.
- Thirty per cent of all UK holiday flights depart from Manchester.

A new terminal is being built.

- The first phase of development will increase the capacity of the airport to 18 million passengers per year.
- The second phase (to be completed by 1998) will increase the capacity to 24 million.

Source E Manchester: an example of airport development

Flying the world

6 You are going to travel from Preston (near Manchester) to visit relatives in Maiduguri, Nigeria. You intend to fly with British Airways from London Gatwick.
a Plan your journey, using Source G and other information on pages 28–33. Give reasons for your choice of route and type of transport.
b Measure the distance of each leg of your journey.
c Draw a time–distance map of your journey, where the length of each line represents the time taken. (The flight from London Gatwick to Lagos takes 5 hours 20 minutes, and from London Gatwick to Kano takes 4 hours 40 minutes. You should estimate the other times.)

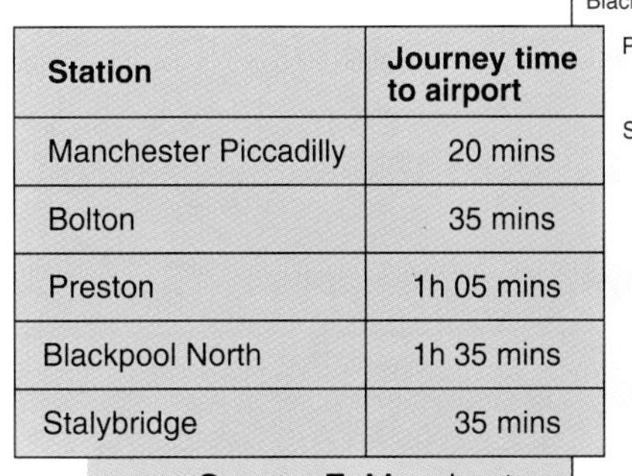

Station	Journey time to airport
Manchester Piccadilly	20 mins
Bolton	35 mins
Preston	1h 05 mins
Blackpool North	1h 35 mins
Stalybridge	35 mins

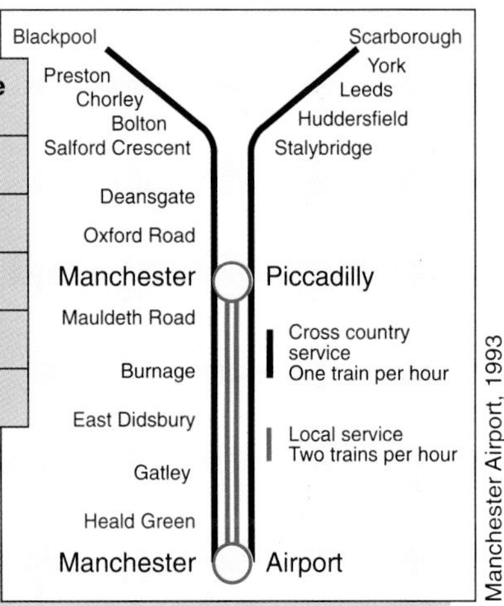

Source F Manchester Airport rail link

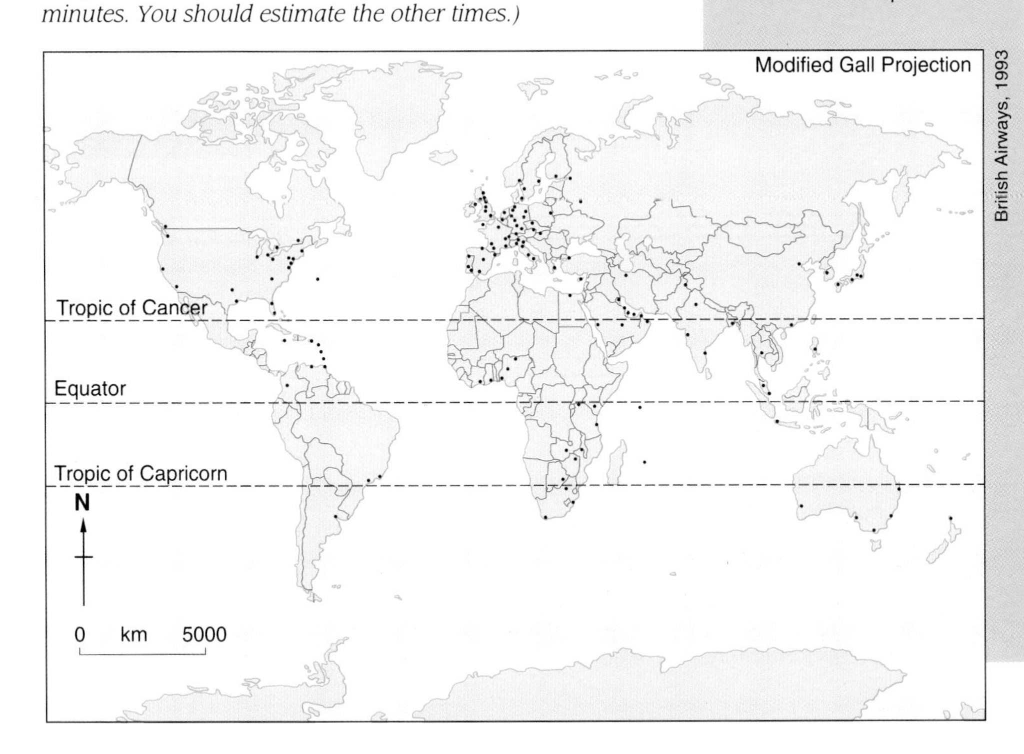

Source G Worldwide destinations, British Airways, 1993

6·1 RURAL AND URBAN NIGERIA

About 65 per cent of Nigerian people live in the countryside. Urban areas are growing rapidly. Why do some settlements grow faster than others? Can cities cope with rapid growth?

Source A Clay bricks are left to dry

Unoka Egboh, head of the household

We have just built another house in our compound for my youngest son who married last month.

We dug clay from a pit during the wet season. When it was thoroughly wet, we trod it into a soft mud and shaped it into bricks. These were left until the weather became drier. My family and friends helped build the walls. It was slow work. Each course of bricks had to be left for a day or two to harden.

I paid carpenters to fit the doors, the windows and the roof frame. The roof was completed with corrugated aluminium which will last longer than the thatch we used to use.

Source B In the Nigerian countryside, it is still usual for houses to be built in the traditional way

Source C The Egbohs' compound in Igboland is an example of traditional, rural housing

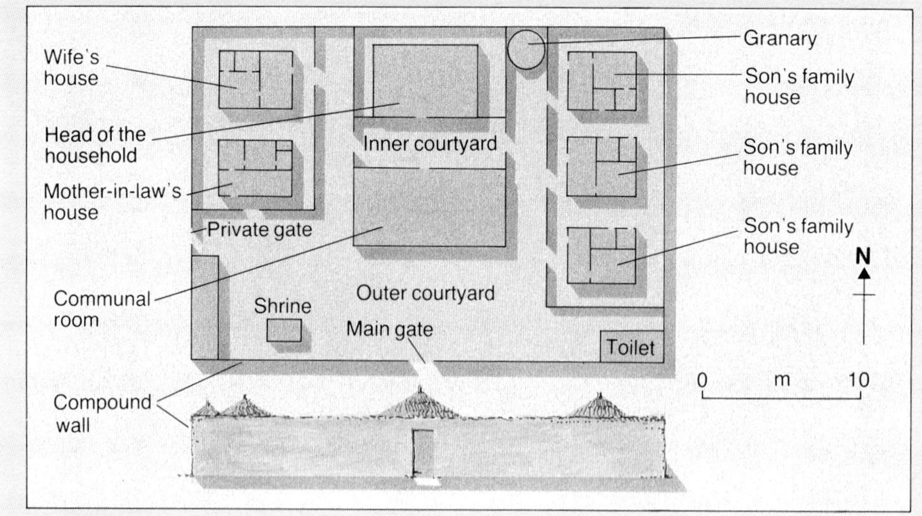

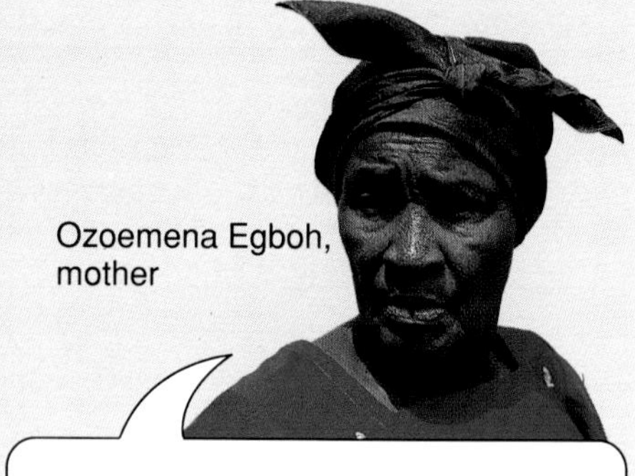

Ozoemena Egboh, mother

In Africa, the household means all the members of the family who eat from the same pot. There are 16 people who live in my household. They include my mother-in-law, my three sons and their families. My daughter, Nneka, moved to Lagos with her family.

The wood we use for cooking makes a lot of smoke, so we cook in the open. If the weather is bad we put up a temporary shelter. Our water supply comes from the stream, as we have no piped water. There is no electricity.

1 Study Sources A,B and C.
a Describe the features of traditional, rural Nigerian homes.
b Explain how the houses are built in this part of Nigeria.
c Suggest why:
- houses have only one storey
- much maintenance is needed.

2 Use the following headings to compare rural Nigerian housing with housing you know:
- Materials used
- Source of materials
- Method of construction
- Size and facilities
- Repair and maintenance needed.

Rural settlement patterns

The style of houses, size of compounds and the pattern of settlement vary across Nigeria. There are, however, three basic types of settlement.

> DISPERSED **houses or compounds**: isolated buildings, usually on the land which the occupants farm.
> HAMLETS: clusters of houses or compounds separated from other groups of houses by farmland, grassland or forest.
> **Villages**: groups of hamlets clustered together and occupied by the same clan. Their population varies between one and five thousand.

Source D Rural settlement

Dispersal of settlements

The traditional settlement in Nigeria is the NUCLEATED village. For defence against hostile tribes or slave traders, most villages were built on the top of a hill or in a bend in the river and were walled.

Over the years, rural settlement has dispersed. This was encouraged by:

- less danger of attack;
- an increase in population, making it necessary to cultivate land further from the settlement;
- better water supplies allowing the IRRIGATION of more land;
- a saving of work time by living closer to the fields;
- the desire to settle more land before neighbouring villages did so.

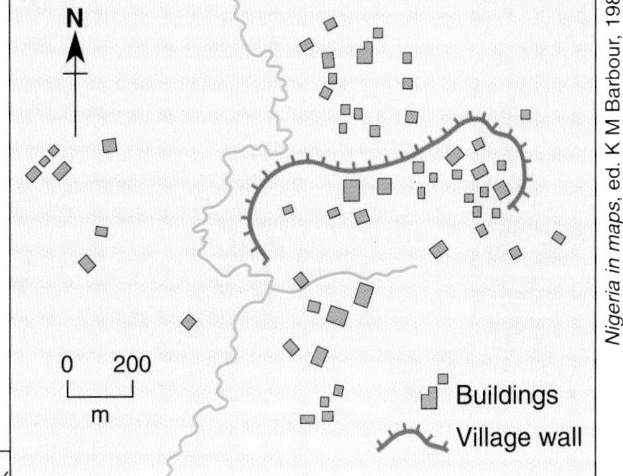

Source E The growth of a village in Igboland, southern Nigeria

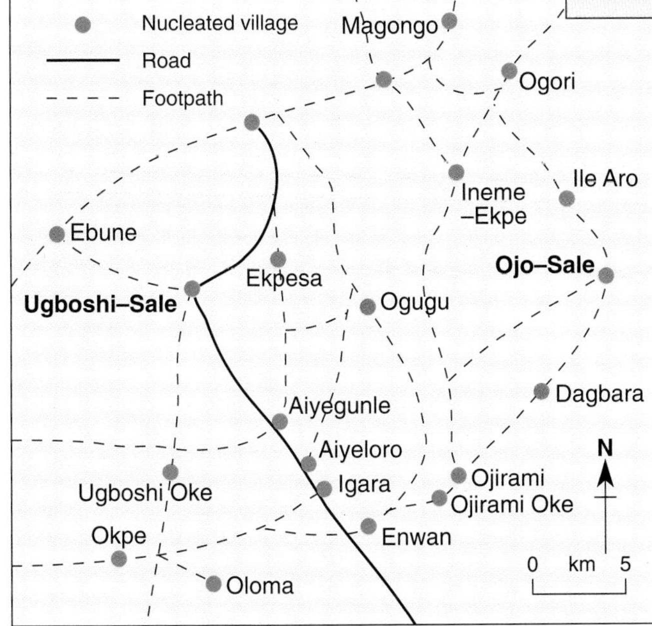

Source F Patterns of rural settlement

3 a Explain what you understand by:
• a dispersed settlement, • a nucleated settlement.
b Study Source D. Describe the scene in the photograph using the terms 'dispersed' and 'nucleated'.
c Suggest the advantages of the two types of settlement.

4 Study Source E.
a Which part of the village do you think was built first? Give a reason for your answer.
b Suggest why the village was built there.
c How has the village grown? State reasons for this growth.

5 Study Source F.
a Imagine you live in Ugboshi-Sale and wish to visit a relative from Ojo-Sale. Describe the journey. Name the villages you would pass through and state the distance you would travel.
b Which do you think is the bigger village of the two? Explain your answer.
c Describe the pattern of settlement in relation to the routeways.

6·2 Going to market

In the economically developed world, many villagers buy goods at a local shop. This is not always true in Nigeria. In rural areas goods are bought and sold in markets.

I go to a market in Igboukwu every four days. I may go to other markets on other days if I have enough to sell. I sell yams or maize depending on the season. If I have a good day I sometimes buy cloth or pottery from another trader. Nowadays, we can usually find IMPORTED *goods such as soap powder at the market.*

Market days enable us to exchange news as well as goods.

Source B Ekwefi Egboh, daughter-in-law, on her way back home from market

SUBSISTENCE FARMING: the farmer grows food for the family.

Surplus produce is sold at market.

Crops grown and sold to the Marketing Board for EXPORT are called CASH CROPS.

Source A Farming life

Ogbunike 3
2 Abagana
Onitsha
4
1
Uke 1
Obosi
R. Niger
Nnobi
A
Igboukwu
4 Orifite
3
4
1 Ekwulobia
Ozubulu 2
N
Numbers give village position in market cycle
0 km 10
Nigeria in maps, ed. K M Barbour, 1982

Source C Four day market cycles in Igboland

1 Study Source B. Describe how Ekwefi Egboh takes her goods to market.

2 Study Source C.

a If Uke market is held on a Monday:

• Which other markets are held on Monday?

• On which day would the next market be held at Uke?

b Ekwefi normally trades at Igboukwu.

• How far does she travel from her compound at A to get there?

• Which other markets might she visit?

c The interval between market days varies from one part of rural Nigeria to another. It is usually between two and four days. Suggest why a market is not held every day in any one place.

3 Describe the scene in Source D and compare it with a market you know.

Source D A small market in rural Nigeria

Development in the countryside

Much has happened in the countryside. In 1976 the Government introduced free primary education for all children and reformed local government. New roads were built and new factories were opened, based on farm products such as brewing and flour-milling. All this activity created jobs in construction, education and the civil service. It affected farming. The older workers stayed on the farms, but the younger ones found new work and farmed part-time.

Source E A new school is built

Source F A modern market, Port Harcourt

Source G A market trader

I have noticed many changes over the past few years. The town is at a junction of two roads which have been improved. Our market is now bigger and sells more goods. Some are produced locally but more come from other parts of Nigeria or from abroad. You can even buy packaged food.

We open nearly every day and have a permanent stall, like a kiosk, which we can lock up. There are now more craftworkers such as carpenters, tailors, bicycle repairers and car mechanics.

In the gossip of the market-place we hear about the higher wages paid in Lagos and other large towns. Many people would like to go there.

4 **a** Describe the changes which have taken place in rural Nigeria since 1976.
b How do you think these changes have helped to change the markets?

5 **a** When Nneka visits her mother, how do you think she might persuade her to think Lagos is an attractive city?
b For what purposes do you think people from rural areas would want to visit a town?

6 *In what ways is the pattern of services in rural Nigeria:*
• similar to, • different from those in a rural area that you know?

6·3 Lagos: a fast-growing city

Lagos has attracted traders from Europe since the fifteenth century. The first to arrive were the Portuguese. (Lagos means lagoon in Portuguese.) They were followed by others, including slave traders for whom Lagos was a major port in the eighteenth century. In 1861 Britain took control of Lagos and from there spread its rule over the whole of Nigeria. Nigeria was a British colony from 1914 until it regained independence in 1960.

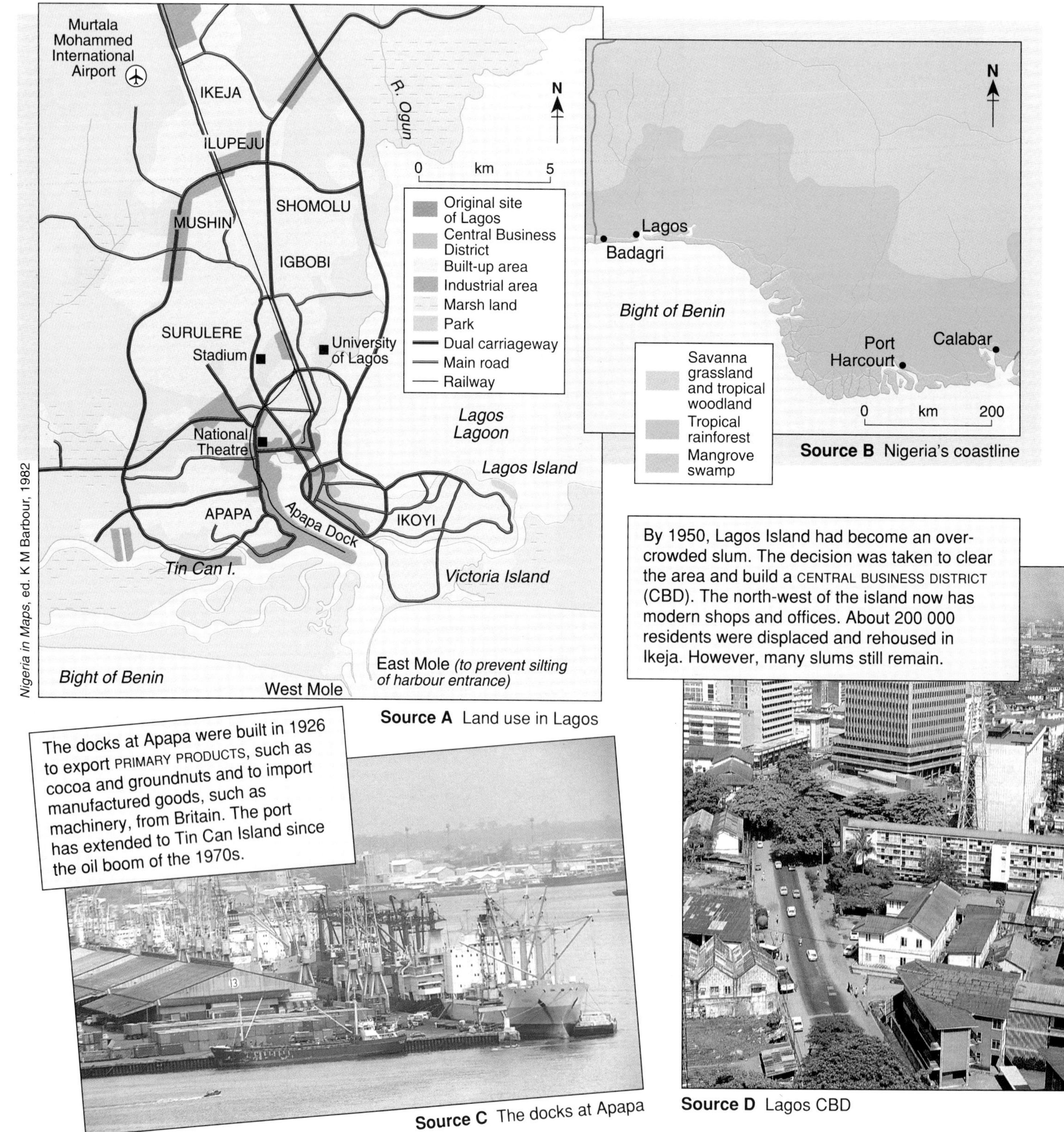

Source A Land use in Lagos

Source B Nigeria's coastline

By 1950, Lagos Island had become an over-crowded slum. The decision was taken to clear the area and build a CENTRAL BUSINESS DISTRICT (CBD). The north-west of the island now has modern shops and offices. About 200 000 residents were displaced and rehoused in Ikeja. However, many slums still remain.

The docks at Apapa were built in 1926 to export PRIMARY PRODUCTS, such as cocoa and groundnuts and to import manufactured goods, such as machinery, from Britain. The port has extended to Tin Can Island since the oil boom of the 1970s.

Source C The docks at Apapa

Source D Lagos CBD

Large numbers of people work on Lagos Island. Residential areas are to the north. The movement of commuters, shoppers and industrial traffic across the city causes a great deal of congestion.

Source E Traffic congestion

NEW ROAD RULES

The Government announced today a scheme to reduce traffic congestion in Lagos. Vehicles with odd-numbered registration plates are to travel on odd days of the month only. Even-numbered vehicles will enter the city on even days.

Source F A scheme to reduce traffic

Well-planned industrial estates have been built in Ikeja, Mushin and Ilupeju. The industry is light and includes food processing, bottling soft drinks, making plastic goods and some engineering. The food, chemical, metal and textile industries are found on larger industrial sites near the docks.

Source G A modern industrial estate

High-class houses were built on Ikoyi and Victoria Island for British colonial officials. The areas were carefully designed. Since 1960, offices and large hotels have been built on the islands.

Source H Victoria Island

1 Study Sources A and B.
a What is the name of the sea area south of Lagos?
b In which direction would a ship travel from the sea to Apapa docks?
c Suggest why a harbour developed at this point.
d In which direction has Lagos grown inland?
e Suggest why Lagos did not expand along the coast.

2 Study Source D.
a Describe the scene in the photograph.
b In what ways is the CBD similar to a town or city that you know?
c Suggest a problem which arises from the CBD being on Lagos Island.
d Imagine you were one of the people who had to move to Ikeja when the CBD was built. Suggest the advantages and disadvantages of the move.

3 Study Sources C and G. Why do you think industry has been located:
- at Mushin,
- at Apapa?

4 Study Source H.
a Describe the scene shown in the photograph.
b In what ways do you think Ikoyi and Victoria Island differ from other parts of the city?

5 Study Sources B, E and F.
a Why do you think traffic congestion occurs in Lagos?
b What is being done to relieve the congestion?
c Suggest other measures which people in Lagos might take to relieve road congestion.
d How do you think the establishment of the new capital at Abuja might be affecting
- *traffic problems in Lagos*
- *the POPULATION DENSITY of Lagos?*

6·4 Lagos: finding a place to live

Large areas of Lagos are unplanned, partly self-built and provide homes for poor people. Many of these are MIGRANTS from rural areas who have come to Lagos to find work.

These people are not SQUATTERS. They are legally entitled to be there. The buildings are not those of a SQUATTER SETTLEMENT. They are solid enough to be permanent and are called 'popular' settlements.

Year	Population
1952	341 500
1963	1 136 000
1974	2 437 300
1976	3 519 000
1982	4 068 500
1984	4 485 600
1991	5 685 800

Source A Population of Lagos State

Source B Popular settlement in Lagos

SWAMP CITY BLUES

... by 1980 ... the government had said it wanted no more migrants (moving to Lagos). Crime and squalor might have kept people away. But the lights were bright and there was money to be made.

The Economist, 20 December, 1986

Source C The attractions of Lagos

One area of 'popular' settlement is Olaleye village. At one time it was a small farming community. It has been swallowed up by the growth of Lagos. It is built on low-lying land. In the east it is swampy and regularly flooded.

1 Study Source A.
a Draw a line graph to show the population growth of Lagos State from 1952 to 1991. (Note that the interval between years varies.)
b Describe what your graph shows.
c What problems might this cause the Lagos Housing Authority?

2 What is meant by:
• squatters, • squatter settlements?

3 Study Sources D and G. About 20 000 people live on 35 hectares of land in Olaleye village. Calculate the population density of the village. How does this compare to other areas of the city?

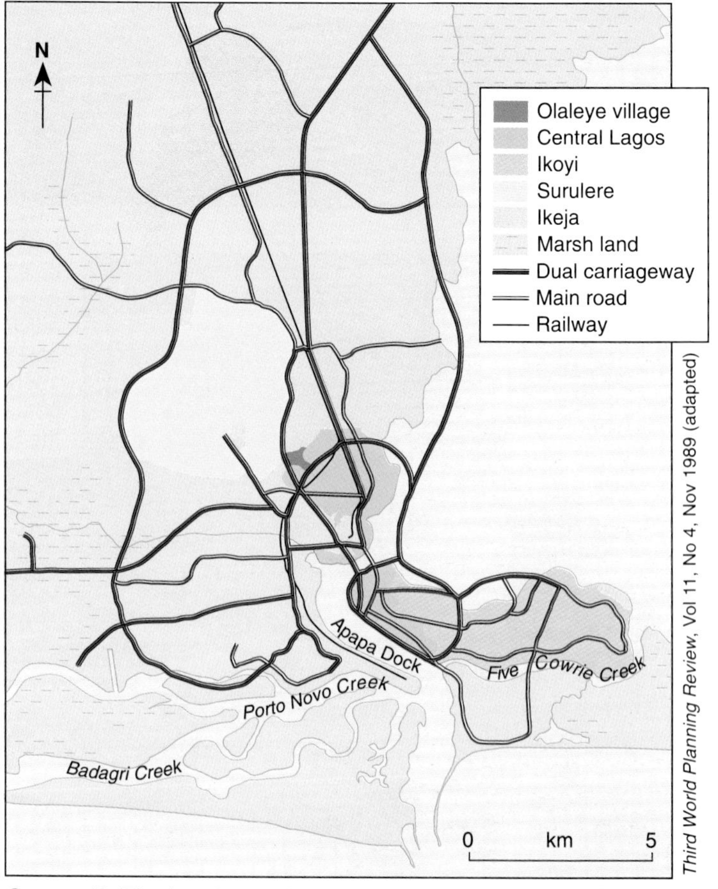

Source D The location of Olaleye village

I moved here with my husband, Yambo, and four children five years ago. The population of our village compound was growing and we could not feed everybody. The cocoa trees were growing old and some were diseased.

I now make baskets and sell them in the local market. Yambo works in a small factory making plastic sandals. Our eldest son did well at school and works in an office on Lagos Island.

I would be happy to return to our village if we could earn enough there. There is more money in Lagos, especially since oil was discovered in Nigeria.

It is not comfortable to live here. We share the kitchen and the latrine with the other two families. There is no piped water or electricity and the only drains are open ditches by the road.

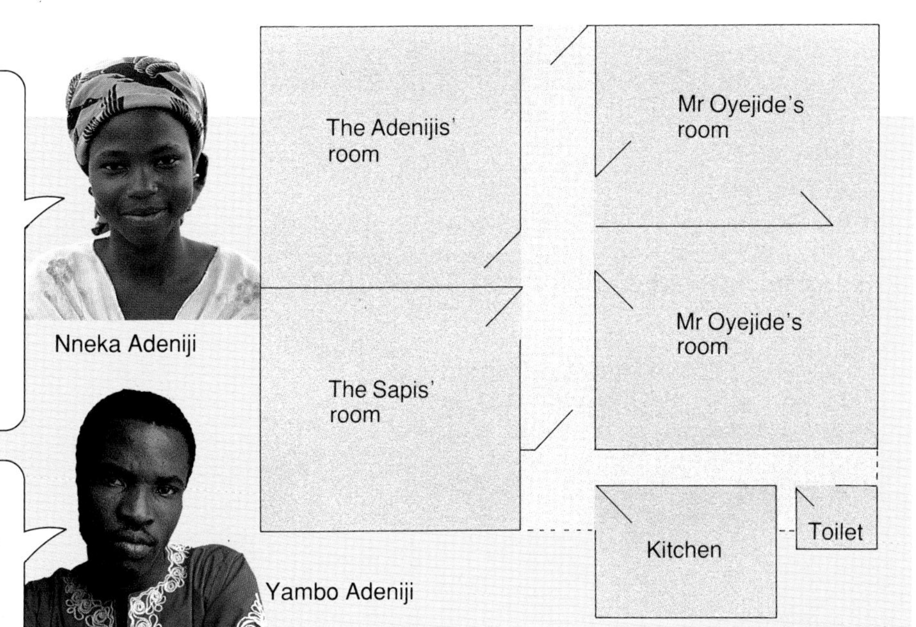

Source E Nneka now lives in a 'popular' settlement in Olaleye village

When I came to Lagos, I rented a piece of land and built a house on it. I built most of the house myself using wood and corrugated iron. I had help to lay the foundations and a carpenter made the doors and window frames for me.

There are 22 people living in my house. Some larger houses have nearly 50. In time, I may add more rooms.

Mr Oyejide, the landlord

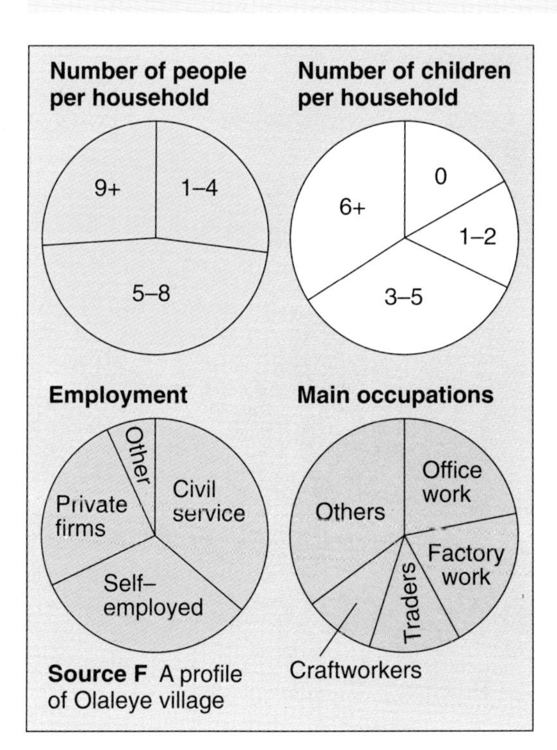

Source F A profile of Olaleye village

	Residential districts in Lagos			
	Central Lagos	**Ikoyi**	**Surulere**	**Ikeja**
Distance from city centre (km)	0	5–6	7–8	16–19
Population density per hectare	1000	35	420–550	175
Percentage of houses with piped water	80	100	30	100
Percentage of tarred roads	30	100	60	100
Main types of houses	Rented rooms	Houses or flats	Houses 40% Rented rooms 50%	Houses

Source G Housing comparisons in Lagos

4 Read Source E.
a Explain why the Adeniji family moved to Lagos.
b In what ways is the housebuilding
• similar to, • different from that described on page 34?
c Imagine you are either Nneka or Yambo Adeniji. Write a letter back to the family comparing your new life in Lagos with village life.

5 Compare Source E with Source F. Are the Adeniji family typical of the area? Explain your answer.

6 Study Source G.
a Rank the four districts, starting with the one with the most comfortable living conditions.
b Explain your decision for numbers 1 and 4.
c How does the rank order compare with:
• the distance from the city centre
• the type of housing found in the district?

7 *Why would the Nigerian government wish to encourage people to remain in the countryside? What strategies might they use to achieve this?*

7·1 TOWN AND COUNTRY

Settlements vary a great deal in size and the services they offer. Why is this? Do the various settlements depend on each other? Is there a pattern of settlements over a large area? How are settlements changing?

Some people live in isolated homes which are a long way from other houses. Many farmers do so. Usually, however, houses are clustered together to form a settlement.

The settlement may consist of just a few dwellings to form a HAMLET. At the other extreme, it may cover hundreds of square kilometres to form a large city.

Four types of settlement

Source A Different settlements in East Anglia

1 Study Source A, which shows a hamlet, a village, a town and a city.

a Describe the scene in each photograph.

b Match each photograph to the settlement type. Give reasons for your choice.

The size of a settlement affects the services it provides

Settlement	Primary school	Post office	Small supermarket	Bank	Secondary school	Shoe shop	Marks & Spencer	University	Population (to nearest 100 people)
Norwich	✓	✓	✓	✓	✓	✓	✓	✓	120 900
Great Yarmouth	✓	✓	✓	✓	✓	✓	✓		47 700
Wymondham	✓	✓	✓	✓	✓	✓			10 900
Stalham	✓	✓	✓	✓	✓				2 800
Mattishall	✓	✓	✓						2 500
North Tuddenham		✓							300

Source B Services provided in selected settlements in East Norfolk

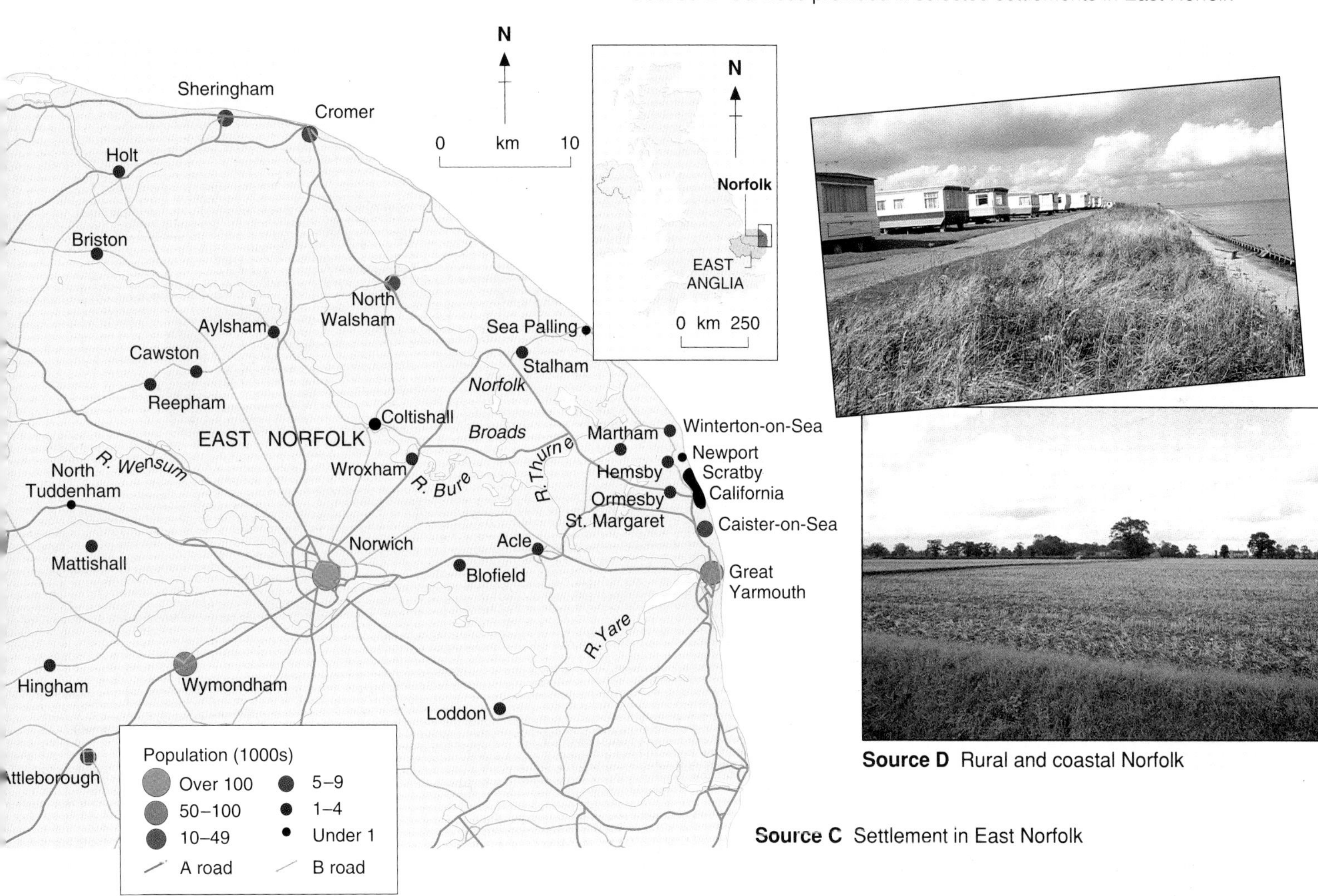

Source C Settlement in East Norfolk

Source D Rural and coastal Norfolk

2 Study Sources B and C.
a What effect does population size have on the services provided by a settlement?
b What is the smallest population which supports:
- a Marks & Spencer store
- a secondary school
- a small supermarket?

c Suggest why there is:
- a primary school in nearly every settlement
- a secondary school only in larger settlements.

3 Look again at Sources B and C. Assume that all places of a similar size provide similar services.
a If you lived in Sea Palling, what is probably the nearest settlement where you could:
- buy baked beans
- go to secondary school
- shop at Marks & Spencer?

In each case, state the distance you would have to travel.
b Why might you go further than your nearest settlement for goods and other services?

4 *Study Sources C and D.*
a *Why do you think there are few large towns in East Norfolk?*
b *Try to explain the presence of fairly large settlements to the north of Great Yarmouth.*

How far do customers travel?

Cheaper goods, shorter distances

Nearly all my customers live in the village. Usually they only want to buy a few small items such as a tin of soup or a packet of frozen peas. It is convenient for them to call in. It wouldn't be worth travelling a long way just to buy one or two things.

The villagers have to travel into town for the more expensive goods, though. It doesn't pay me to stock these.

Mr Davidson,
village shopkeeper

We sell most electrical goods. They can be expensive, and people don't buy them very often. To have enough business, we must attract customers from a wide area. The shop is in the centre of town which people can reach easily. They don't seem to mind coming a long way to buy expensive goods. In the town they are able to compare the prices of our goods with those of other electrical suppliers.

Ms Visagie,
manager of an electrical store

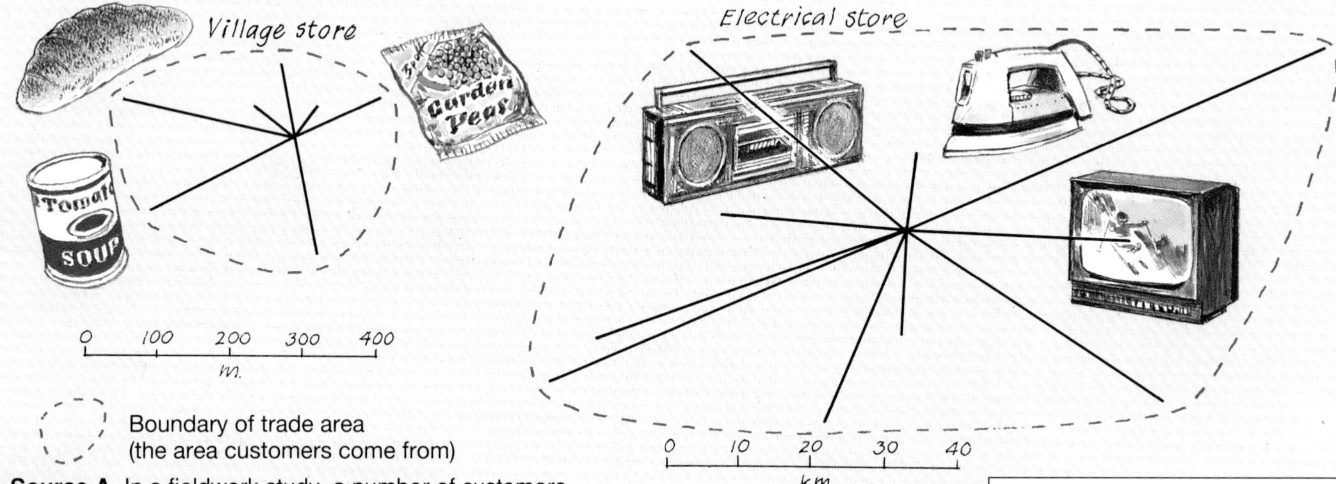

Source A In a fieldwork study, a number of customers at a village store and an electrical store in town were asked where they lived. Lines were drawn from their homes to the stores

Goods or services	Bought or used				Where last bought or used
	Daily	Weekly	Monthly	Less often	
Newspaper					
Butter/margarine					
Washing powder					

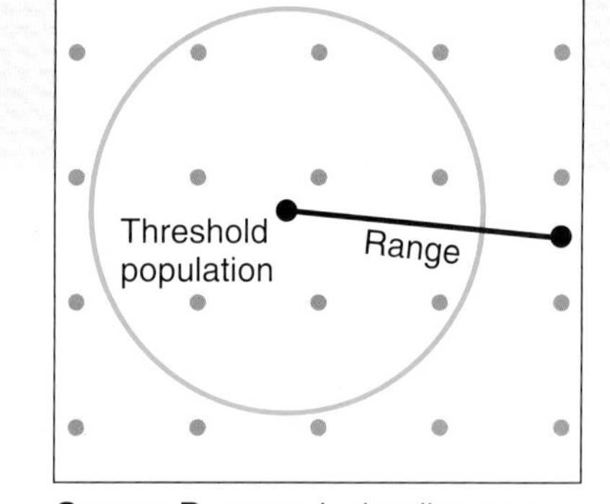

Source B RANGE is the distance a customer is prepared to travel for a particular item or service. THRESHOLD POPULATION is the smallest number of customers necessary to support a service

1 Copy the table above.
a Add dry cleaning, shoes, shirt, electric kettle and cinema to the list.
b Write down how often you or your family buy the goods or use the service.
c State where you or your family last bought the goods or used the service.

2 Study Source A.
a What is the greatest distance a customer travelled to reach:
- the village shop
- the electrical store in the town?

b Try to explain the difference between the two distances.
c Why might a town have many small supermarkets but few electrical stores?

3 Study Source B.
a If each dot represents 50 people, what is the threshold population of this shop?
b Draw a diagram for a shoe shop with a threshold population of 5000 customers. Decide on a scale.

Are times changing?

Shopping habits began to change in the 1970s when self-service supermarkets were opened. They changed further in the 1980s when hypermarkets and regional shopping centres were built away from towns and city centres.

Source C The new hypermarket on the outskirts of Wymondham

Source D The development of out-of-town hypermarkets threatens village shops

Shoppers	Norwich	Small town	Village	Elsewhere
Elderly people	8	29	60	3
Women with a driving licence	14	44	40	2
Women without a driving licence	7	32	61	0

Source E The percentage of people using shopping centres for convenience goods. The survey looked at three categories of shoppers in rural Norfolk, 1985

Reason	%
Price too high	31
Work in town and shop there	27
Limited stock choice	18
Others	24

Source F The reasons people gave for not using their local shops. Taken from a survey in rural Norfolk, 1985

Villages in decline

When I first moved to the village there were five shops, six pubs, a doctor's surgery, a hair-dresser and a shoe repairer. Now there are two shops, both self-service, and two pubs. To visit our doctor we have to go to a clinic in the next village. The nearest chemist is 10 km away. Many people have cars, so the travel does not bother them. I have to rely on the bus service, which is infrequent and expensive.

I read in our local paper that 600 shops were closed in rural Norfolk between 1951 and 1980, as well as 50 surgeries and 50 primary schools.

Source G Charles Anderson, villager

4 An item or service with a short range and a small threshold population is said to be LOW-ORDER. It is bought regularly and is cheap. An item with a long range and a large threshold population is HIGH-ORDER. It is more expensive than a low-order item and is bought less often.

a Look at Source A. State whether the village store and the electrical shop sell low- or high-order goods.

b Add a third column to your table called low- or high-order. Complete the column for each of the goods and services.

c *Why do you think low-order goods are sometimes called* CONVENIENCE GOODS *and high-order goods are known as* COMPARISON GOODS*?*

d *Settlements which sell high-order goods and services can be called high-order centres. How would you expect the number and spacing of high-order centres to compare with low-order centres in an area?*

5 Study Sources C, D, E and F.

a Why do you think large hypermarkets are popular with shoppers?

b How do the shopping habits of women drivers compare with those of women non-drivers and the elderly? Give reasons for your answer.

c Why do you suppose there are protests about the opening of new hypermarkets away from town centres?

6 Read Source G.

a What effects have the changes in services had on villages?

b Why do you think surgeries and primary schools have closed?

7·3 Settlements grow and change

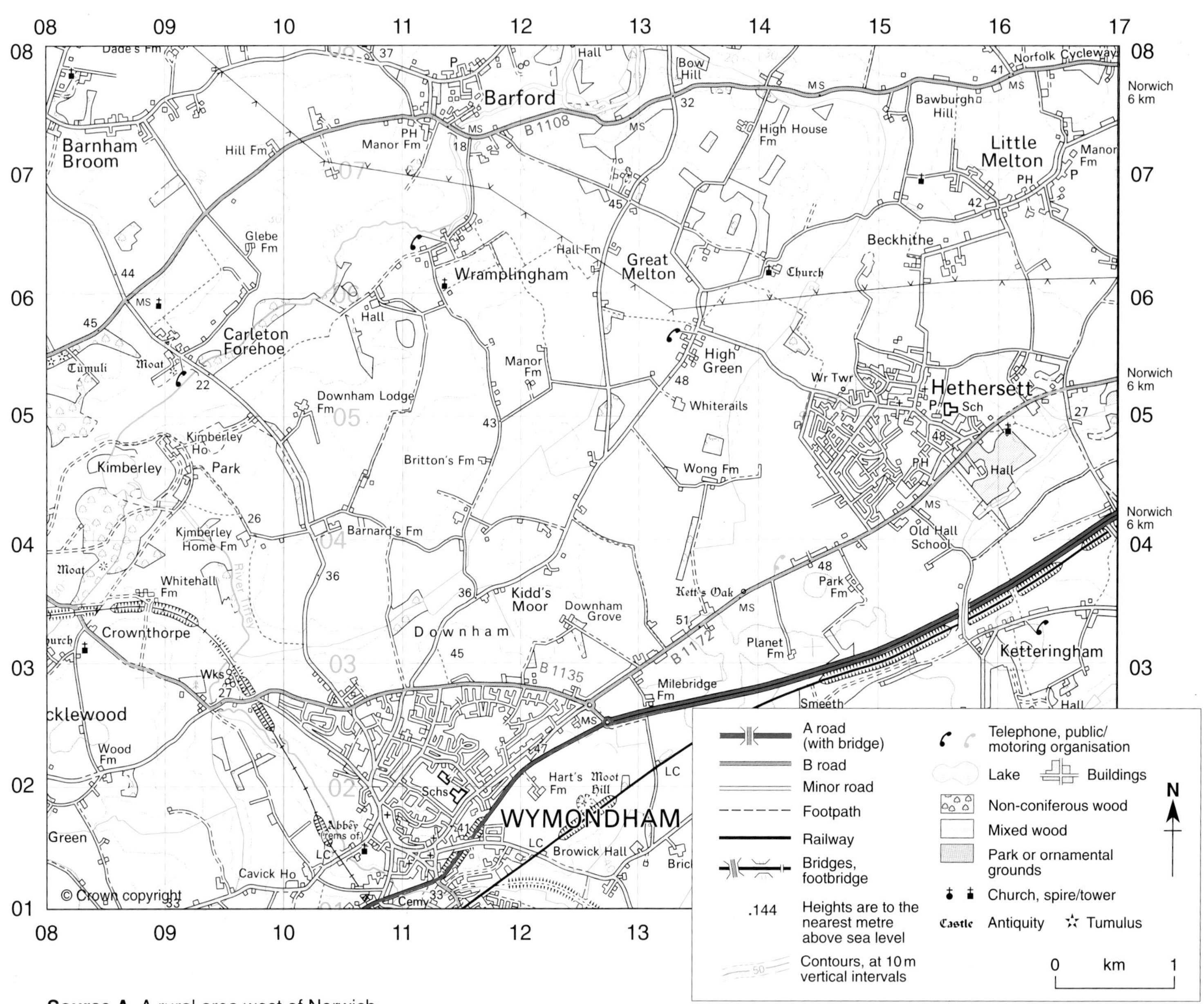

Source A A rural area west of Norwich

1 Study Source A. A hypermarket has recently been built at grid reference (GR) 126025.

a Name an A and a B road which meet near the hypermarket.

b Suggest two reasons why the hypermarket was built there.

2 Jean and Graham Blythe live near Barford village store. However, they now shop at the hypermarket.

a Write down:
- the four-figure grid reference for Barford
- the straight-line distance between Barford and the hypermarket
- the direction of the hypermarket from Barford.

b Using the map, Jean describes their journey to the hypermarket: 'We join the B1108 at GR 112074, where we travel west. We drive for about three kilometres passing Hill Farm on the right, GR 099072. At the crossroads, GR 087059, we travel south-east'.

Describe the rest of Jean and Graham's journey. Include grid references for the features that they pass, such as the bridge, woodland and road junctions.

c What is the distance of their journey? How much shorter is the journey Jean and Graham could take through Wramplingham, GR 1106?

d Suggest why Jean and Graham do not use this route.

e Many people from Hethersett use the hypermarket. Suggest why they might prefer to buy low-order goods there rather than in: • Hethersett, • Wymondham, • Norwich.

3 Using Source A:

a Name two examples of NUCLEATED settlement.

b Give an example of DISPERSED settlement.

Village	1931	1941	1951	1961	1971	1981	1991
Barford	253	—	292	297	375	384	425
Hethersett	1241	—	1413	1613	3034	4172	4624
Wymondham	5017	—	5665	5904	8480	9813	10869

Source B Population change

Hethersett	Barford
Primary school	Primary school
Secondary school	Public house
Public house (×3)	Garage
Garage (×2)	Store
Bakery/tea shop	Vehicle hire shop
Post office	
Bank	
Library	
Chemist	
Chinese takeaway	
Newsagent	
Florist	
Upholsterer	
Hotel/B & B	

Source C Services available in Barford and Hethersett

1

2

3

Source D Views of Barford and Hethersett

The Norfolk Structure Plan provided for 990 houses to be built in Hethersett between 1981 and 1996, and for the A11(T) road to be straightened and widened between Hethersett and Norwich.

4 Copy and complete the table below to compare Barford and Hethersett.

Feature	Hethersett	Barford
Area built on		
Shape		
Height above sea level		
Slope of land		

5 Study Source B.
a Draw line graphs to compare the populations of Barford and Hethersett between 1931 and 1991.
b What do the graphs tell you about the populations?
c Suggest why no figures exist for 1941.

6 **a** Suggest why Hethersett was chosen as a village which should grow.
b What might be the views of each of the following about the growth of Hethersett:
- an elderly villager,
- a local farmer
- a newcomer who has moved from Norwich?

c *Why do you think Hethersett could not be called a town?*

A Central Business District

The centre of a town or city is called the CENTRAL BUSINESS DISTRICT (CBD). It is a distinctive part of the city, quite unlike any other district.

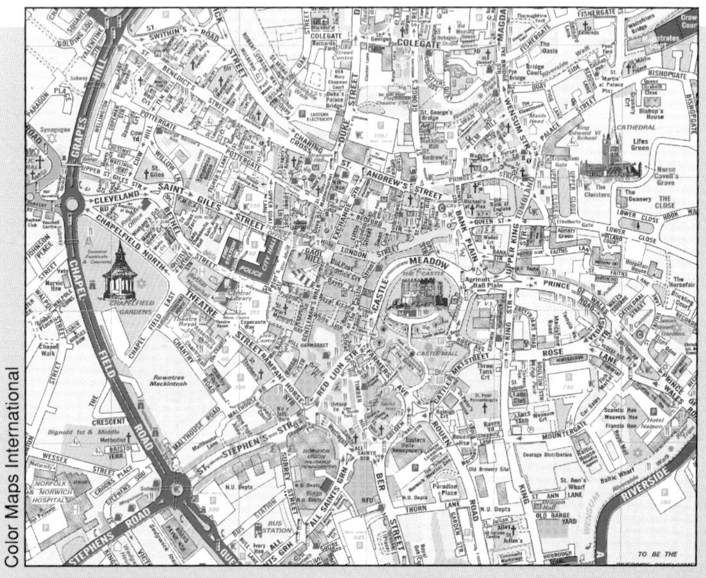

Color Maps International

Source A Part of a tourist information map of Norwich CBD

Source B St Stephen's Street, Norwich

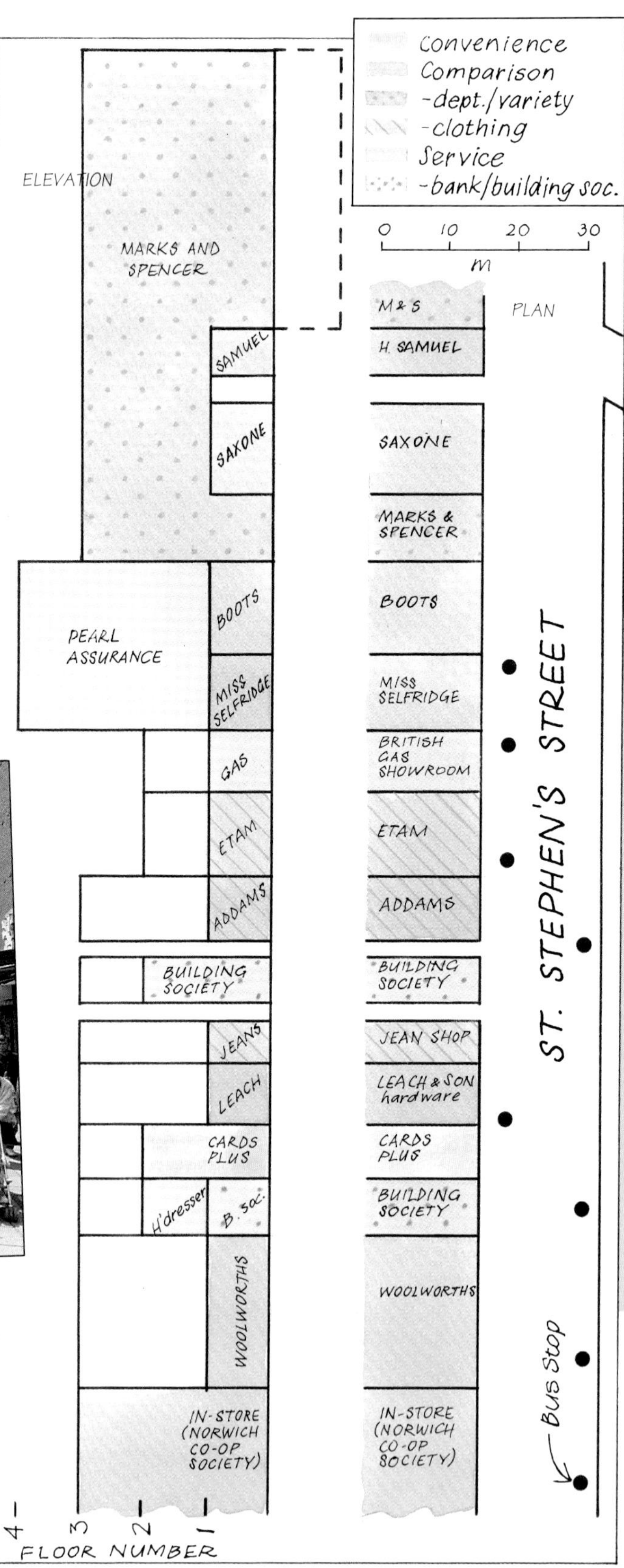

Source C Results of a student's mapping survey on the use of buildings in part of St Stephen's Street, Norwich

1 Study Source A.
a List at least three pieces of evidence that this is a map of a city centre.
b State three functions of the city centre shown on the map.

2 Study Sources B and C.
a Name six shops which are found in the centre of a town or city that you know.
b Why do you think many buildings in the city centre are several storeys high?
c State two ways in which upper floors of buildings are used.

Source D London Street, Norwich

Source E Results of a student's mapping survey on a section of London Street, Norwich

Source F Distribution of shops and services in Norwich CBD

Shops	Number (%)	Floor space (%)
Convenience	10	8
Comparison	55	63
– department	(4)	(26)
– clothing	(15)	(13)
Service	25	19
bank/building soc.	(7)	(9)

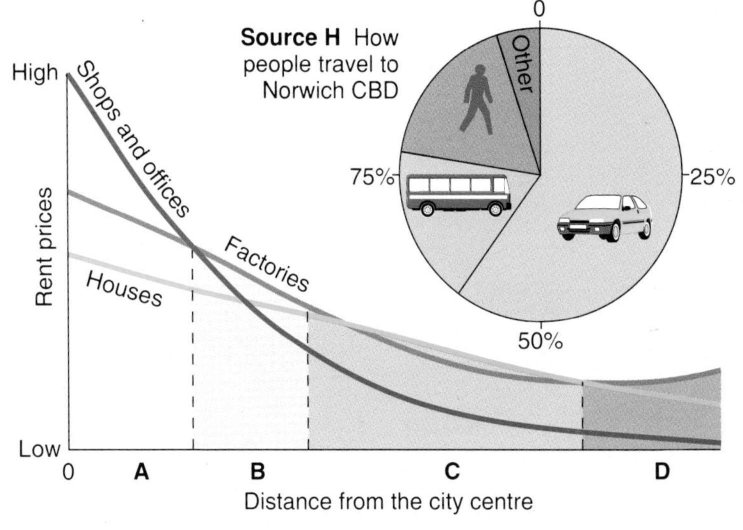

Source H How people travel to Norwich CBD

Source I Land use across a city

How often do you shop in Norwich?

Answer	% response
Every day	7
2–3 times a week	24
Once a week	52
Less often	17

How far do you have to travel to reach the centre of Norwich?

Answer	% response
0–1 km	22
2–5 km	34
6–10 km	26
Over 10 km	18

Source G Results of students' questionnaires on Norwich shoppers

3 Study Sources B, C, D and E.
a Compare St Stephen's Street and London Street under the following headings:
• streets, • size of shops, • type of shops.
b Suggest why London Street has been closed to traffic?
c Suggest why many shoe shops and clothes shops are found close to each other?

4 Study Source F.
a Draw divided bar graphs to show the percentage of shops which are convenience, comparison and services according to: • number, • floor space. (10 per cent are vacant.)
b Describe the graphs and explain any differences between them.

5 **a** Draw appropriate graphs to illustrate the information in Source G.
b Describe and explain the main features of each graph.

6 Study Source H.
a What percentage of people travel to Norwich CBD
• by car, • by bus, • on foot?
b Explain the high percentage of car users.
c Suggest what methods of transport might be included under 'other'.

7 Study Source I.
a How does the price of land change as you move away from the city centre?
b Describe the type of land use you would expect to find in the four areas, A to D.
c Suggest why owners of shops and offices are prepared to pay a high rent for a location in the city centre.

8·1 BELFAST – A TROUBLED CITY

Belfast has grown in a similar way to other British cities and has a similar pattern of land use. It is, however, deeply divided by religion. How did this come about? What have been the geographical effects of this division?

Source A A 'peaceline' dividing Catholic and Protestant housing

How did division arise?

1534 King Henry VIII established the Church of England. Ireland remained loyal to the Catholic Church.

1600

1607 Catholic leaders were defeated in battle. Protestant settlers from England and Scotland were given large areas of confiscated land in the north of Ireland. Irish Catholics were pushed to poorer lands in the south.

1641 Catholic rebellion. This was crushed by Oliver Cromwell who arrived in 1649. Catholics lived as inferior citizens outside Protestant towns.

1700

1798 Some Protestants united with Catholics to rebel against British rule. They were defeated.

1800

1801 Act of Union Ireland became part of the United Kingdom. The Act was opposed mainly by Catholics who wanted an independent Ireland, but was supported by most Protestants (Unionists) who wanted links with Great Britain.

1846 Famine killed over one million people in Ireland. Many people emigrated abroad or moved from the south to the north of Ireland.

During the nineteeth century, Belfast became an industrial city and port. Catholics moved to the city to find work.

1886 and 1893 Attempts to achieve Home Rule for Ireland legally were defeated in Parliament.

1900

1916 Easter Rising rebellion defeated, but support for Sinn Féin grew.
1919 Irish Republican Army (IRA) established as anti-British underground freedom fighters.

1919–21 Civil War in Ireland to regain independence.
1920/21 Ireland was divided into two separate states. Northern Ireland and the Irish Free State were both under British government control.

1922 The Irish Free State became independent from Britain.

1949 The Republic of Ireland came into existence.

1967 The Civil Rights Association formed to stop discrimination against Catholics.

1969 Severe conflict between the Protestant and Catholic communities led to the moving in of a British army peace-keeping force.

1969 'The Troubles' The IRA have given violent support to the Catholic Nationalists. The Ulster Defence Association (UDA) have done the same for the Protestant Unionists.

1972 Northern Ireland government abolished and replaced by direct rule from Westminster.

Source B History of the division

1 Study Source A.
a Describe the 'peaceline'.
b Why do you think it was built?
c Describe the housing area in which it is built.

2 Study Source B. Describe the conflict between Catholics and Protestants: • before 1700, • between 1800–1921, • after 1921.

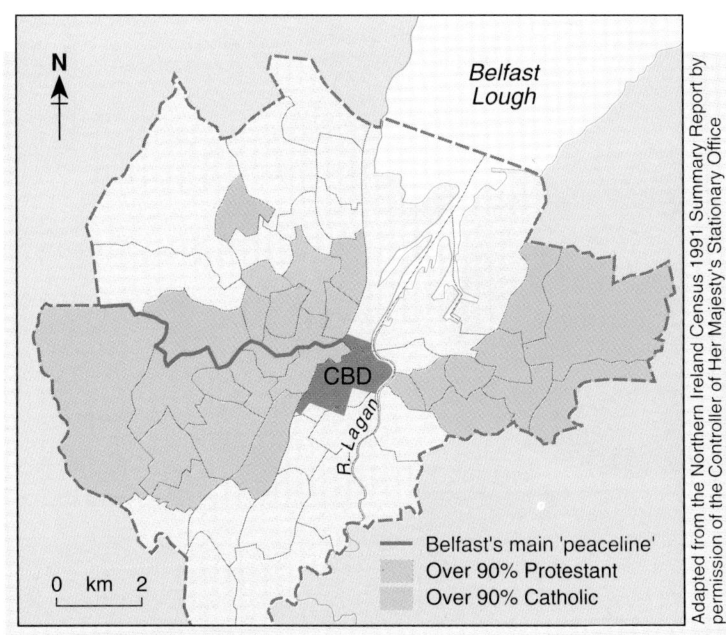

Adapted from the Northern Ireland Census 1991 Summary Report by permission of the Controller of Her Majesty's Stationary Office

Source C Divisions in Belfast's population, 1991

Most people live separate lives according to their religion. They shop in segregated shopping centres, drink in segregated bars and their children attend segregated schools.

Breda Quinn, a taxi driver

Brent Corbett, a student

I'm Protestant and my girlfriend is Catholic, and we live in neighbouring houses in the suburbs near the university. It's a quiet area and there's never been any bother.

Of course, I see the soldiers on patrol in the city centre, but I've never seen a gun used. Belfast's crime rate is quite low. There are places in Belfast I wouldn't go, but that applies everywhere.

Source D Different opinions

Grand Opera House bombed

May 1993

Two killed in Ulster

A part-time soldier with the Royal Irish Regiment was killed yesterday when an IRA bomb exploded beneath his car. He was the second terrorist victim in 15 hours.

The first was a Roman Catholic living in a predominantly Protestant estate on the outskirts of Belfast who was shot dead as he watched television. He had lived in the area for 23 years.

John Mullin, *The Guardian*, 1 June 1993

JOBS APARTHEID IN UK'S RELIGIOUS ENCLAVES

The unemployment rate in Northern Ireland is 14.2 per cent. However, the most recent Labour Force survey shows that 18 per cent of Catholics are unemployed against 8 per cent of Protestants.

Queens University, Belfast has signed a declaration that it intends to achieve equality. At present only 28 per cent of its workforce are Catholic.

Mary Holland, *The Observer*, 18 April 1993

Source E Newspaper coverage of the 'Troubles'

Source F The Cornmarket, Belfast city centre

Separate communities

3 Study Sources C and D.

a Describe the distribution of Catholics and Protestants in Belfast.

b How do the opinions of Breda Quinn and Brent Corbett differ?

c Suggest reasons why they hold such different opinions.

d What evidence is there that the communities are reluctant to integrate?

4 Study Source E. In what ways are people in Belfast suffering as a result of division?

5 Study Source F. Suggest why a PEDESTRIANISED street is safer in Belfast for: • shoppers, • shopkeepers.

8·2 The growth of Belfast

An industrial city

The original site of Belfast was at the lowest crossing point of the River Lagan. A bridge was built in 1688.

In the eighteenth century, water power from fast-flowing TRIBUTARIES of the River Lagan was used in the bleach mills. People moved to Belfast from rural areas.

Source A Belfast: the development of industry

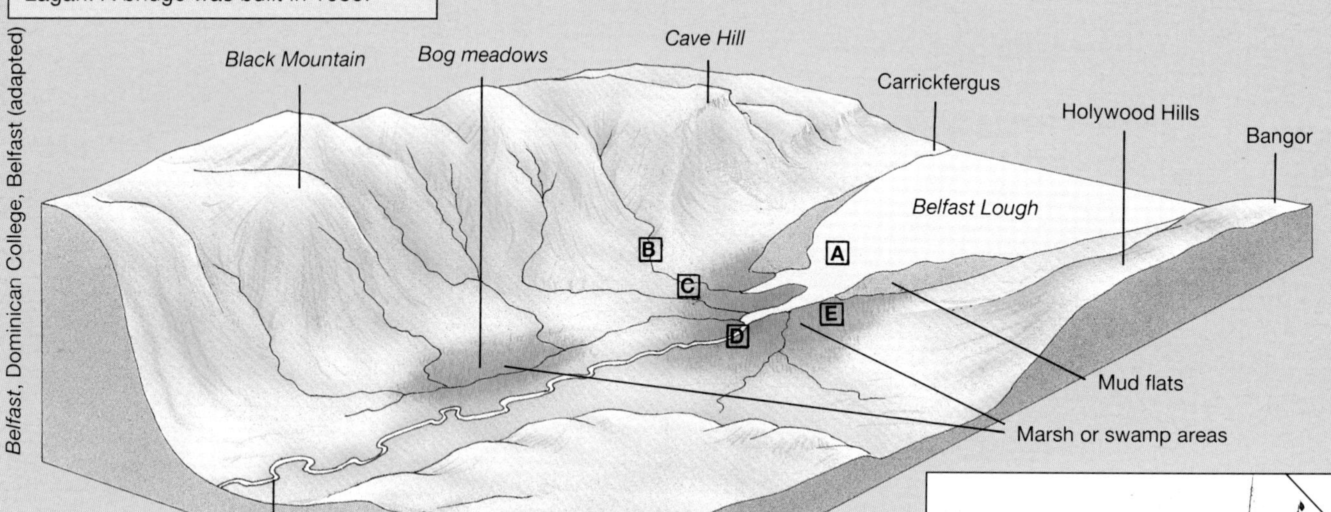

The original site of Belfast

Belfast, Dominican College, Belfast (adapted)

In the nineteenth century, a deep water channel was dredged in Belfast Lough. Large ships could dock. Coal was IMPORTED from England.

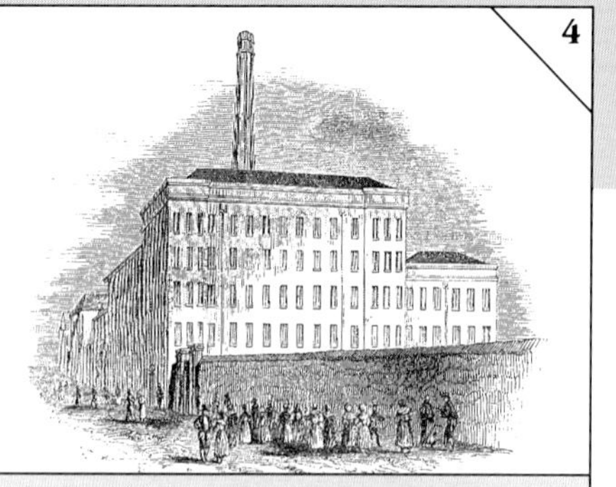

In 1824 the first factories were built in Belfast for spinning and weaving locally grown flax to make linen. Linen was EXPORTED worldwide and by the late nineteenth century had a huge American market.

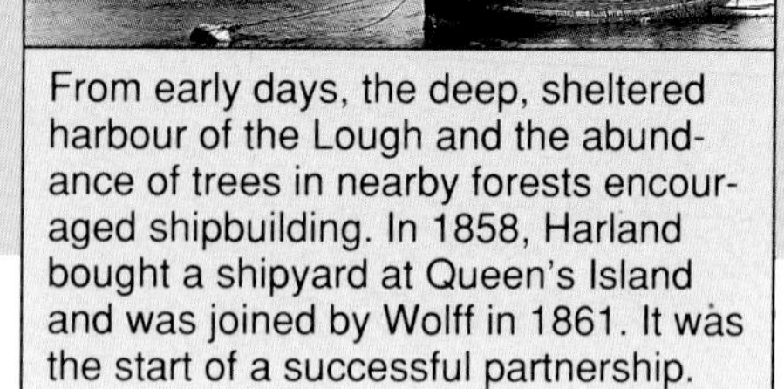

From early days, the deep, sheltered harbour of the Lough and the abundance of trees in nearby forests encouraged shipbuilding. In 1858, Harland bought a shipyard at Queen's Island and was joined by Wolff in 1861. It was the start of a successful partnership.

1 Study Source A.

a Describe the site of Belfast. (The site is the land on which it is built.)

b Match pictures 1–5 with the areas A–E marked on the diagram.

c State three features of Belfast which made it a suitable location for industry.

d Draw and label a time line to show the development of industry in Belfast.

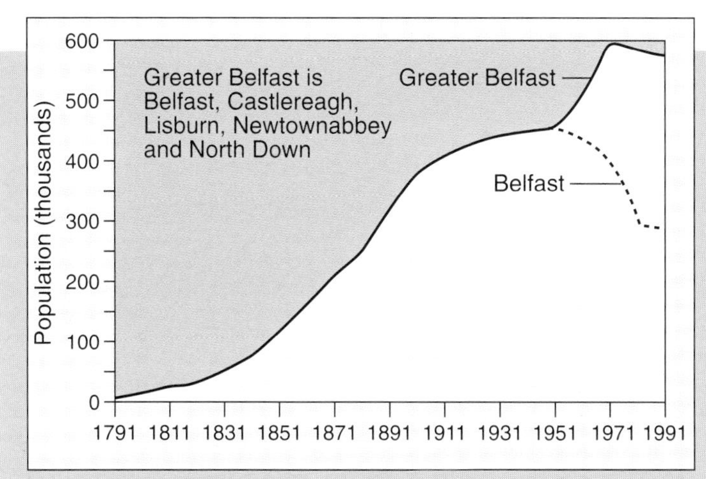

Source B Belfast's population, 1781–1991

Year	Birth rate per 1000	Death rate per 1000
1600	35	34
1700	38	37
1801	36	25
1901	28	19
1926	23	15
1951	21	13
1961	22	11
1971	20	11
1981	18	10
1991	17	10

Belfast, Dominican College Belfast

Source C Belfast: birth and death rates, 1600–1991

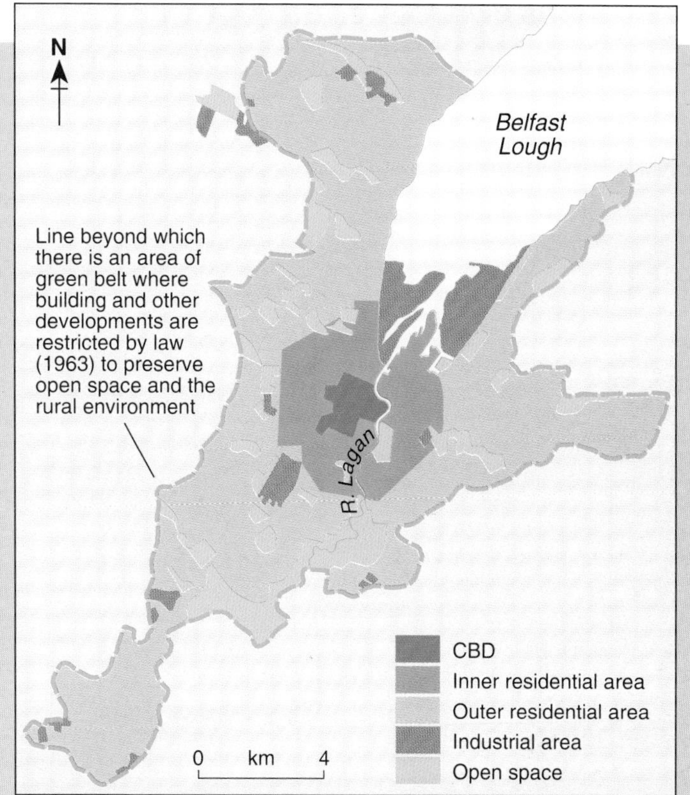

Source D Belfast: land use

Source E Belfast: industry and history

2 Study Source B.
a Describe the changing population of Belfast: • up to 1971, • after 1971.
b Compare population growth with your time line of industrial development.

3 Study Source C.
a Draw two line graphs to show the BIRTH RATE and DEATH RATE of Belfast between 1600 and 1991.
b Shade the area between the two lines and label it 'population growth' by natural increase.
c Describe the main features of your graph.
d What factors, other than NATURAL INCREASE (birth rate minus death rate), can affect the total population?

4 Study Sources D and E.
a Describe the shape of Belfast.
b How is the shape related to the site (Source A)?
c Where would you expect to find the two scenes shown in Source E?
d Describe the pattern of land use in Belfast.

8·3 Planning for security

Housing in Belfast

In 1971 the Northern Ireland Housing Executive was set up to take responsibility for housing. It was non-political. Its PLANNERS had to redevelop Belfast's housing and try to reduce conflict between Protestants and Catholics.

Source A The Belfast housing problem

Nineteenth century housing consisted of sturdy two-up, two-down terraces. When they were built they were of good quality, but by 1970 they were in bad repair. Little housing had been built in the inter-war years. The post-war slum clearance programme had not been very successful. Many houses had poor amenities. Large areas were derelict.

The housing situation was made worse by the 'Troubles' after 1969. There was much intimidation. Whole streets were burned. Between 1969 and 1976, up to 60 000 people had been forced to move within or out of Belfast because of sectarian violence. They wanted refuge in their own areas.

Building a better Belfast, N Ireland Housing Executive

Source B Redevelopment of old terrace housing

Source C A move to the suburbs, 1970s

Source D Poleglass housing estate, West Belfast

1 Study Source A and look at Source C, page 60.
a Suggest what rooms would be found in a two-up, two-down terrace house.
b What modern facilities might it not have had?

2 a List three things which had happened to inner-city housing by 1965.
b Suggest how the 'Troubles' altered the housing situation.
c What effects did this have on where people lived?

3 Study Source C.
a Make a list of Protestant and Catholic areas of inner-city Belfast.
b From which of these areas have people moved? In each case, say where they have moved to and whether it was an inner-city or outer-city area.
c Suggest why new housing was built in the outer city.
d What effect might such movement have on the 'Troubles'?

4 a Draw a sketch map of Source D. Show the road pattern, housing and other land uses.
b Label your map to show the area's most important features.
c Discuss with a partner the advantages and disadvantages of living in this area compared with that shown in Source B. Share your ideas with the rest of your class.

The redevelopment of Ballymacarrett

Ballymacarrett is an inner-city housing area redeveloped in the 1980s. There has always been segregation between Catholics and Protestants. However, during the 1960s, there was some integration. This changed with an outbreak of violence in October, 1969. The mixed areas on either side of Newtownards Road, Albertbridge Road and Bryson Street disappeared. Houses were abandoned and vandalised or destroyed. Sectarian divides (divisions based on differences of religious belief) became established.

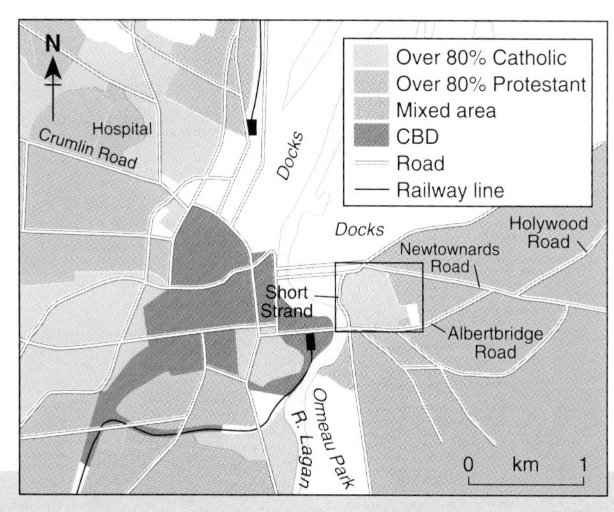

Source E Ballymacarrett: the background to redevelopment

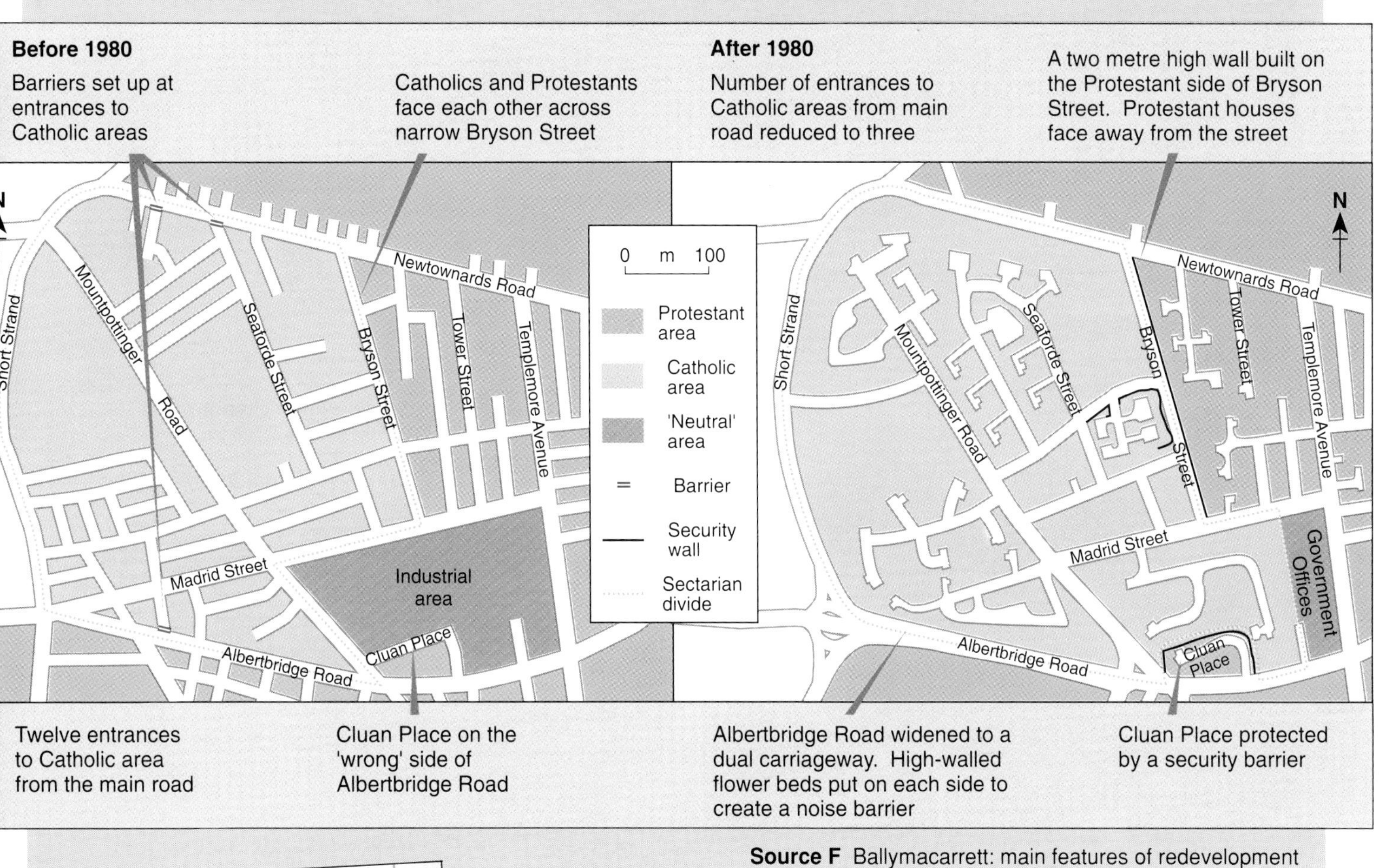

Source F Ballymacarrett: main features of redevelopment

Source G Environmental barriers on the Crumlin Road

5 Using Source E:
a Write three sentences to describe the location of Ballymacarrett.
b Estimate the size of the area.
c How did the area change in 1969? What were the reasons for these changes?

6 Study Source F.
a Describe the land use pattern of Ballymacarrett before redevelopment.
b How did redevelopment change the road pattern?
c How does the new road pattern compare with that shown in Source D?
d Suggest how the changes shown in Source F may have affected safety with regard to: • traffic, • sectarian violence.

7 Study Sources F and G.
a Describe the scene in the photograph.
b Why has redevelopment demanded an environmental barrier?

8 *Do you think it is better to redevelop an inner-area in Belfast or to rehouse people in outer-city housing estates? Give reasons for your answers.*

8·4 How is Belfast changing?

Population

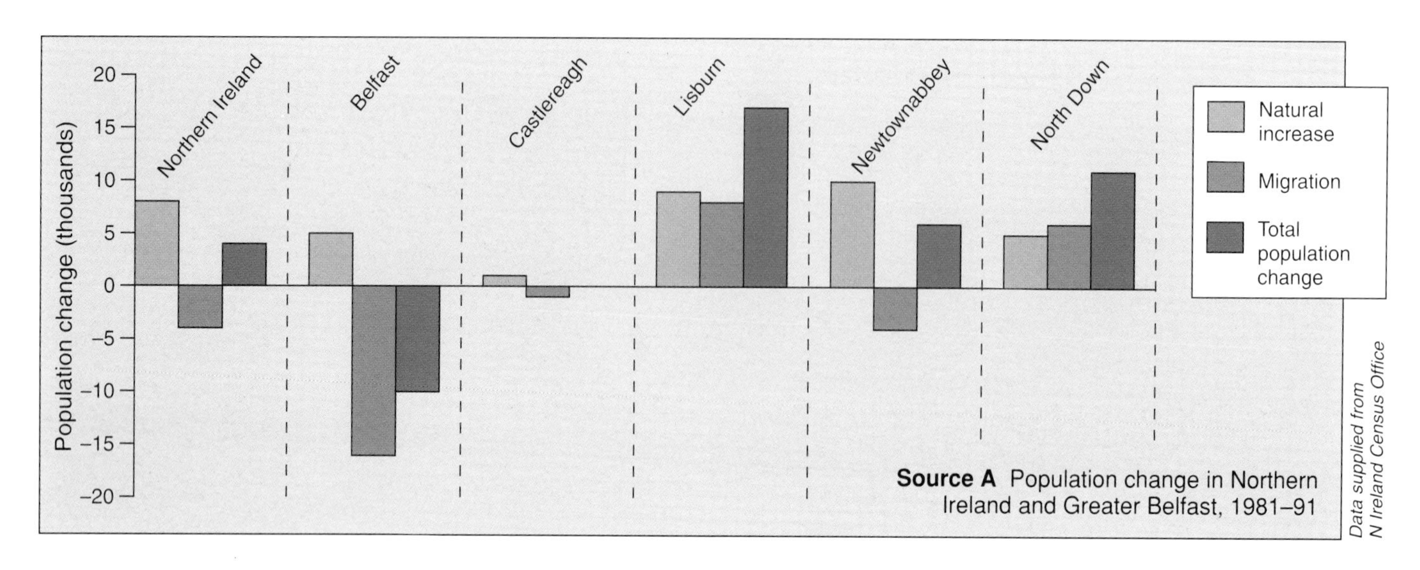

Source A Population change in Northern Ireland and Greater Belfast, 1981–91

Data supplied from N Ireland Census Office

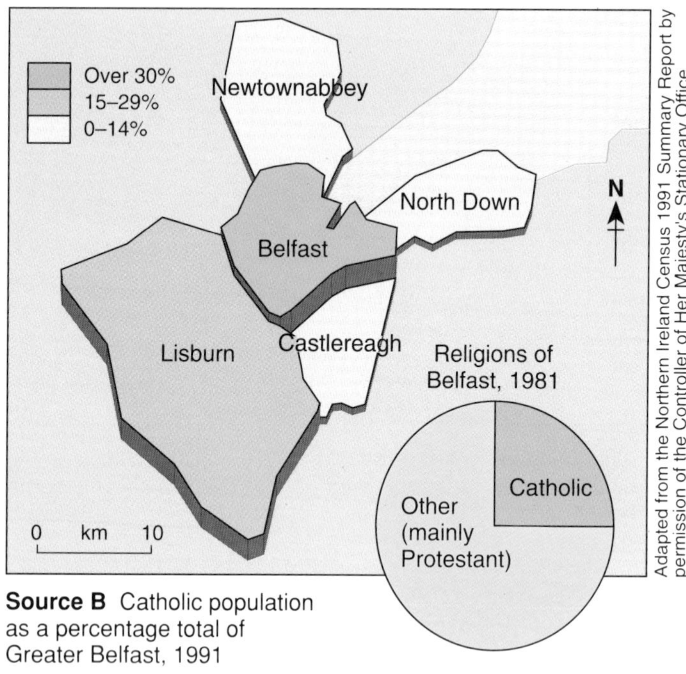

Source B Catholic population as a percentage total of Greater Belfast, 1991

Adapted from the Northern Ireland Census 1991 Summary Report by permission of the Controller of Her Majesty's Stationary Office

1 Study Source A.

a Copy and complete the table below:

District	Population change (%) 1981–91		
	Natural increase	**Migration**	**Total**
N. Ireland	+7.5	−4.5	+3.0
Belfast			
Castlereagh			
Lisburn			
Newtownabbey			
North Down			

Give your table a title.

b What do you notice about the: • change by natural increase, • total change?

c Which districts gained by MIGRATION during 1981–91?

The Guardian, 17 May 1993

Population drift risks Unionist grip on Belfast

A HUNDRED YEARS of Unionist (Protestant) control of Belfast city council could end this week when council elections in Northern Ireland are expected to produce greater support for power-sharing.

The predicted shift in fortunes is chiefly due to gradual population changes. Catholics are now estimated to constitute around 42 per cent of Northern Ireland residents, a figure which rises to 50 per cent among those of school age.

In Belfast the drift has been accounted by many Protestants moving from the city centre to suburbs to the north and east which lie in other council areas.

Source C Council elections, May 1993

2 Study Source B.

a Describe the pattern shown by the map.

b How did the Catholic population of Belfast change between 1981 and 1991?

3 Study Source C.

a Suggest two reasons why the percentage of Catholics in Belfast is likely to rise.

b How might this affect the political control of Belfast?

Employment

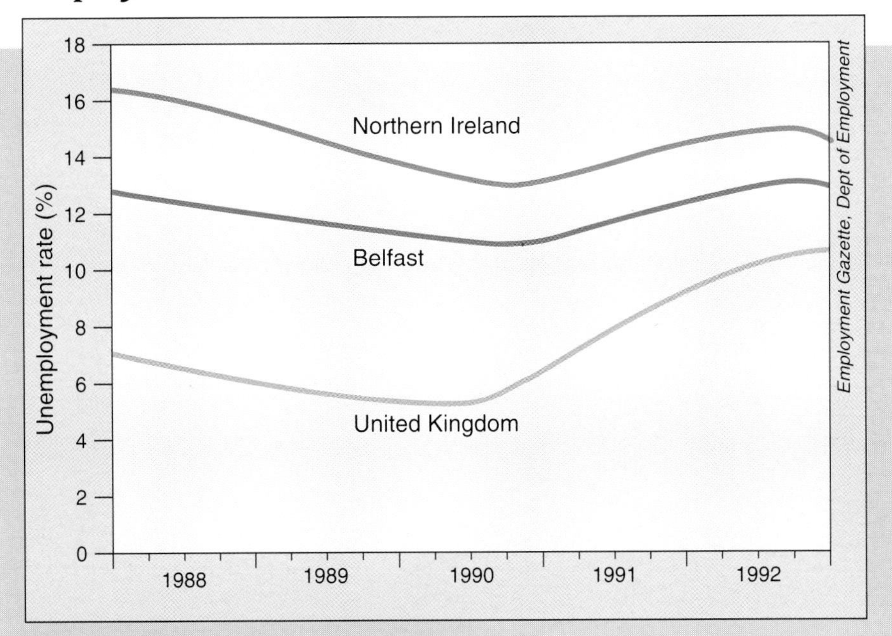

Source D Changing unemployment, 1988–93

Harland and Wolff were once famous for building passenger ships, included the unlucky 'Titanic' in 1912. Through both world wars they worked on naval vessels. Demand for passenger ships fell sharply in the 1950s and 60s, and the yard was re-equipped to build huge oil tankers and bulk carriers. It was successful in spite of severe competition from countries such as Japan. Gradually however, orders became fewer and the shipyard lost money. Today the shipyard still builds tankers and ferries, but also general engineering equipment such as for off-shore gas and oil rigs, weirs and bridges.

Year	Number employed at Harland and Wolff
1959	20 000
1969	12 000
1982	7 000
1989	5 000
1993	3 000

Source E The Harland and Wolff shipyard

Source F British Airways reservations office

Unemployment and poverty are commonplace in Belfast. On certain estates everyone is unemployed. The fortunes of Harland and Wolff, once a major employer, are sinking, but they had a reputation for only employing Protestants. Today, job prospects are bleak for all young people. I can no longer tell my pupils they must work hard to get a good job.

Mrs Rhodes Mr Haywood

I think part of the answer to our problems is integrated schooling. This is difficult, but some parents do not want their children to go through school without meeting anyone from the opposite side. At present there are two primary and two secondary integrated schools in Belfast. The children get on well, but sometimes find it awkward visiting each other's homes. They might meet somewhere in the city centre, like MacDonald's.

Source G Headteachers' comments

4 Study Source D.
a State the highest and lowest *employment* percentage between 1988 and 1992 for: • Belfast, • Northern Ireland, • the United Kingdom.
b Write a statement to describe changes in each of the following:
- unemployment in Belfast
- unemployment in Northern Ireland.

c Compare these with UK unemployment.

5 Study Source E.
a Draw a line graph to illustrate the numbers employed at Harland and Wolff between 1959 and 1993.
b Describe what your graph shows.
c Suggest why there was a fall in demand for:
- passenger ships in the 1950s
- oil tankers in the 1970s.

6 Study Source F.
a British Airways now have a ticketing office in Belfast. They find it cheaper than London. Suggest reasons for this.
b Explain why the workers who have been made redundant at Harland and Wolff are unlikely to be employed in the British Airways' offices.

7 Study Source G.
a Explain what is meant by an 'integrated school'.
b Do you think integrated schools help to solve the problems of division in Belfast? Explain your answer.
c There are proposals for two further integrated primary schools in Belfast. Do you think they will become widely established? Use information from pages 50 to 57 to help you explain your answer.

9·1 BIRMINGHAM: LIVING IN A CITY REGION

Great efforts have been made to improve the quality of life for people living in Birmingham. How has the city coped with its problems? How does Birmingham provide for the needs of its multi-ethnic population?

Tracey Porter

Birmingham is a great place to live. There's lots to do. The shopping is brilliant! There is a wide range of shops to suit everyone's tastes. There is the National Indoor Arena and the National Exhibition Centre. There are also museums, theatres and art galleries. It is, however, still difficult to find a job, especially if you've just left school.

Kim Roberts

Birmingham is an attractive city. There are many parks and woodland areas. There are many small and friendly neighbourhoods. Within each, the people have different backgrounds and this makes the city a lively and interesting place.
It's great for music: the City of Birmingham Symphony Orchestra, UB40 and Bhangra groups.

Source A Faces of Birmingham

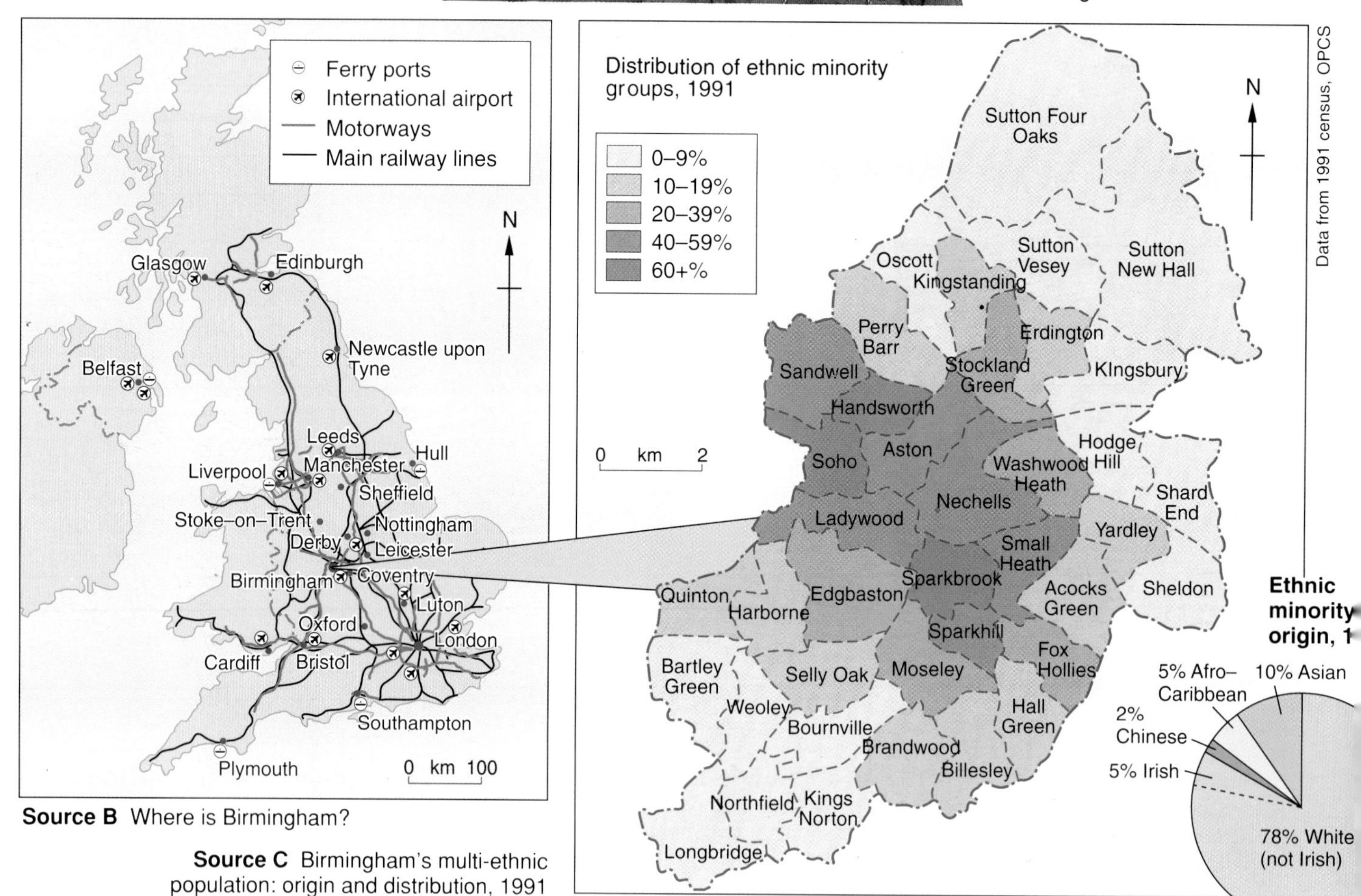

Source B Where is Birmingham?

Source C Birmingham's multi-ethnic population: origin and distribution, 1991

1 Using Source A, list some of the attractions to be found in Birmingham.

2 Study Source B.
a Describe the location of Birmingham within the UK.
b How ACCESSIBLE is Birmingham from:
• London, • Glasgow, • Belfast,
• Cardiff? Explain your answer.

3 Study Source C.
a Describe the distribution of ETHNIC MINORITY populations in Birmingham.
b What other information about ethnic minority groups is not shown on the map?
c What percentage of Birmingham's population is from one of the four main ethnic minority groups?
d Suggest reasons why the Irish community should be regarded as a separate ethnic group.

Population size
Total: 961 041
Females: 495 936
Males: 465 105

Place of birth	Percentage
UK	86
Commonwealth	9.5
European Community	0.5
Rest of the world	4.0

Age group	Unemployment (%) (UK average = 18.9%)
18–19	32.4
20–24	26.6
25–44	16
45–59	14.6

Source D The population of Birmingham, 1991

City scenes

Source E Faces of Birmingham

4 Study Source D. Draw graphs or charts to show:
• Birmingham's population by gender, • places of birth,
• the percentage of unemployment according to age.

5 Study Source E.
a In pairs, make a list of city facilities shown in the photographs.
b Rank the photographs, putting first the one with features you consider most important for a good QUALITY OF LIFE.
c Compare your order with another pair. Give reasons to explain any differences.

6 *Using all the sources, write two or three sentences to summarise your views about Birmingham.*

9·2 Sparkbrook: inner-city redevelopment

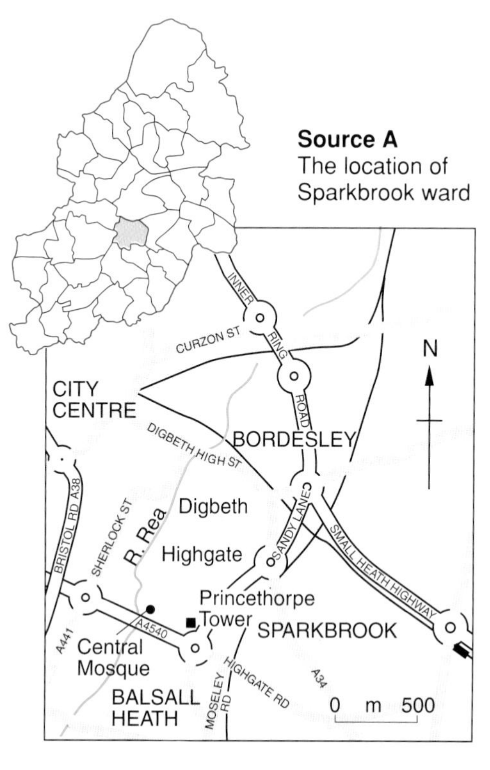

Source A The location of Sparkbrook ward

Comprehensive redevelopment

During the 1960s, the Victorian courtyard housing in Birmingham was replaced by high-rise blocks of flats and later, low-rise housing. PLANNERS decided on a COMPREHENSIVE REDEVELOPMENT scheme. Residents were moved to flats on outer-city council estates while inner-city areas were cleared and completely rebuilt.

Source B The inner-city rebuilt

Courtyard housing

The yard was paved with blue bricks which were slippy in the rain. Each house had two rooms upstairs and two downstairs. The staircase went between the two rooms.

There was a sink in the back room downstairs. It had only cold water. Hot water was from two large, black kettles on the kitchen hob.

Coal was stored in a dimly lit cellar below the front room. Lighting was largely from gas lamps and the gas meter was also in the cellar.

Source C Belgrave Road, 1962

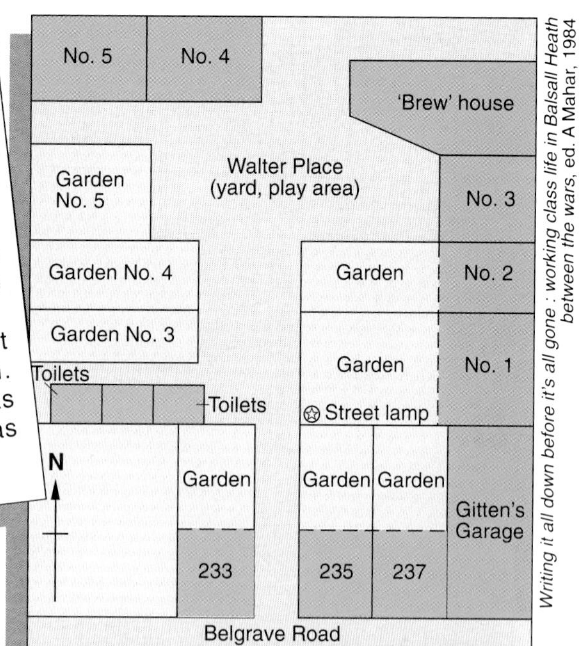

Writing it all down before it's all gone : working class life in Balsall Heath between the wars, ed. A Mahar, 1984

1 Study Source A. Describe the location of Sparkbrook ward within Birmingham.

2 Study Source B. Draw a labelled landscape sketch to show the phases of redevelopment in the inner-city. Mark on your drawing:
- areas of high-rise development
- areas of low-rise housing
- important features of the landscape that you can identify clearly.

3 Study Source C. Although they were moving to new housing, many older residents complained about leaving family and friends.

a Describe how courtyard housing allowed a community spirit to develop.

b What difficulties might the residents have found with their new high-rise flats?

4 *Study Source C. Imagine that you were an Environmental Health Inspector in 1962. Write a short report on your visit to Belgrave Road.*

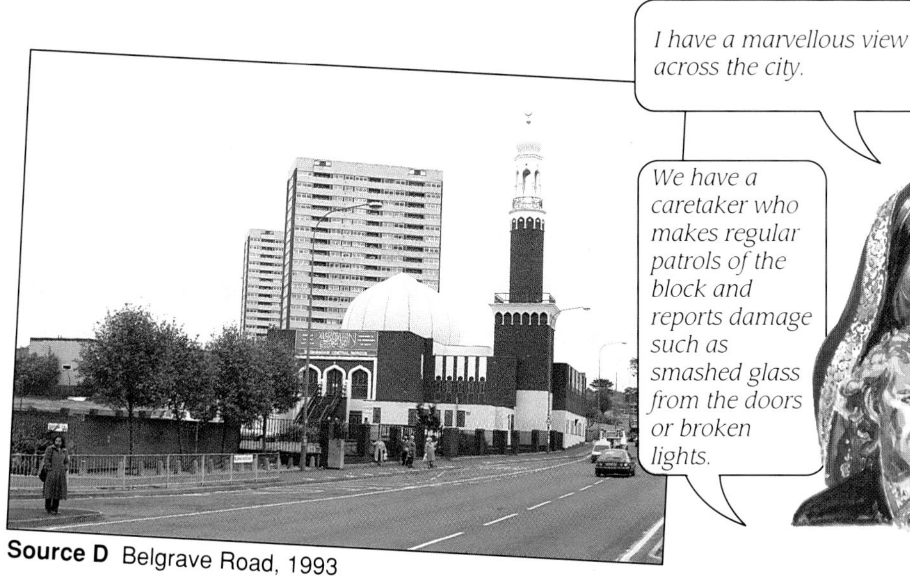
I have a marvellous view across the city.
We have a caretaker who makes regular patrols of the block and reports damage such as smashed glass from the doors or broken lights.
The lifts are always out of order. Try getting a week's shopping and a pram to the 13th floor!
I feel much safer since the Council fitted security coded doors on the ground floor. It's become quieter too.

Source D Belgrave Road, 1993

Source E High-rise flats: residents' views on living in Princethorpe Tower

Ethnic origin	Percentage
White	32
Afro-Caribbean	11
Black African	1
Other Black	2
Indian	7
Pakistani	30
Bangladeshi	8
Chinese	1
Other Asian	2
Irish	1
Others	5

Source F Sparkbrook: population census, 1991

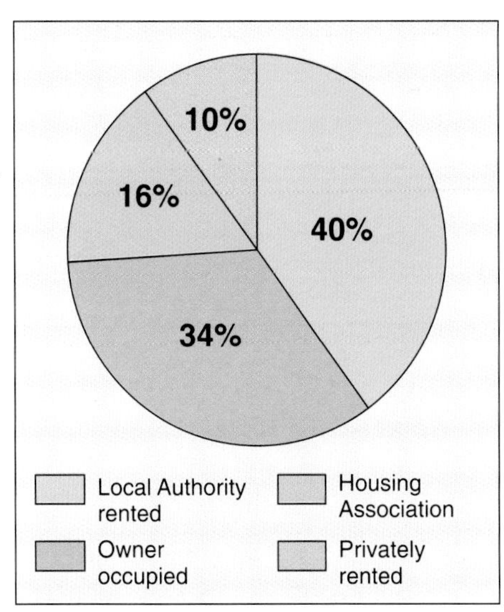
10%
16%
40%
34%
Local Authority rented
Housing Association
Owner occupied
Privately rented

Source G Sparkbrook: patterns of tenure, 1991

Quality of the environment

Students from a local school interviewed residents of the Sparkbrook high-rise flats and low-rise housing. Their survey found that:

- Most of the elderly people enjoyed living in the area.
- Families felt they had better security if they lived in a cul-de-sac, rather than in the flats or houses on the main roads.
- Parents living in the flats wanted safer playgrounds for their children, and for the Council to be better at keeping up the repairs.
- Noise from parties was the most common complaint about neighbours, but this was a minor difficulty.
- On the whole, most people thought that the area was a good place to live.

Positive	+ Average −	Negative
Beautiful		Ugly
Ordered		Chaotic
Rich		Poor
Interesting		Boring
Quiet		Noisy
Friendly		Hostile
Clean		Dirty
Dense		Empty
Like		Dislike
Relaxed		Tense
Successful		Unsuccesssful
	3 2 1 0 1 2 3	

Source H Measuring quality of life, 1962

5 Study Sources C, D and the text.
a Suggest ways in which Belgrave Road today is both similar to and different from how it was in the past.
b In pairs, list the present-day problems facing the residents.
c Suggest possible ways of solving the problems you have identified.

6 Study Source G.
a Discuss what is meant by each of the HOUSING TENURE types.
b Write a short paragraph to describe the pattern of tenure in Sparkbrook.

7 Study Source H.
a Use a copy of the diagram and mark on it your views about the quality of life in Belgrave Road today.
b Compare your graph with the data for 1962.
c Write a short paragraph to summarize the changes that have occurred in this area.

Small Heath: inner-city regeneration

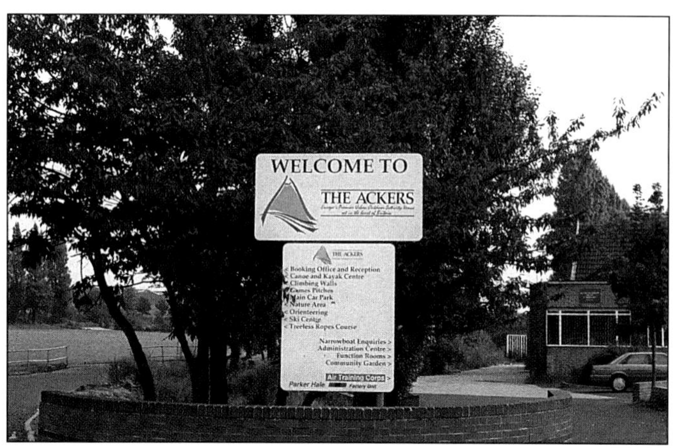

Source A 'The Ackers', Small Heath: probably Britain's largest inner-city recreational complex

Source B Asda superstore, Small Heath

A 'General Improvement Area'

In the 1970s and early 80s, the Small Heath community was devastated by factory closures. Unemployment soared. The local motorcycle industry was destroyed by foreign competition. Electrical components plants were moved to bigger, GREENFIELD SITES on the edge of the city. Local and national governments combined to regenerate the area. Small Heath was declared a 'General Improvement Area'. This meant that new plans were needed to encourage the local economy, increase job opportunities, improve housing conditions and clear the barren waste-land that covered most of the district.

Source C Small Heath: a district plan

1 Study Sources A and B.
a 'The Ackers' and the Asda superstore were built on derelict land. For what other purpose might the land have been used?
b What were the causes of factory closures?

2 Study Source C. You have been asked by the local planning department to explain the Small Heath district plan to geography students. Summarise the main features of the plan under the headings: • Housing, • Industry, • Leisure, • Transport, • Other services.

The 'envelope scheme'

Birmingham City Council had very little money, so planners drew up an 'ENVELOPE SCHEME' for Small Heath. Houses that were basically sound were not knocked down. Instead they were improved, streets at a time. Families moved to friends or relatives, or had everything replaced around them. New roofs, floors, staircases and windows were put into every home. The Council were able to repair three houses for the cost of building one new home.

Waverley Road, during renovation

Waverley Road, after renovation

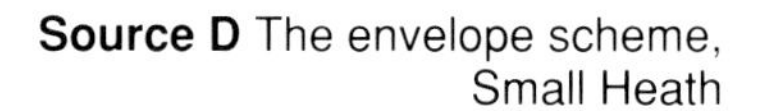

Source D The envelope scheme, Small Heath

A growing community

Year	Population
1971	25 825
1981	21 886
1991	30 470

Source E Small Heath: population change, 1971–91

Place of birth	Percentage
UK	67
Republic of Ireland	4
Commonwealth	28
Caribbean	2.6
Bangladesh	3.6
India	2.5
Pakistan	18.0
Other Asian	1.3
Rest of the world	1.0

Source F Small Heath: population census, 1991

When the Council had completed their programme of housing renovation, they started to clear the derelict land. Working with Housing Associations, the City Council produced low-cost housing for Small Heath's rapidly growing population.

7%
13%
19%
61%
Owner occupied
Privately rented
Local Authority rented
Housing Association

Source G Small Heath: patterns of tenure, 1991

Source H New communities: Housing Association property

3 Study Source D.
a In pairs, discuss the problems of living in a house while it is being improved.
b Why might some residents have objected to changes planned for their home?
c Imagine that you work for local radio or television. Record an interview with a resident from Waverley Road. Cover events from the day they received the news that their house was to be renovated, to its completion.

4 Study Sources E and F.
a Draw a line graph to show population change in Small Heath between 1971 and 1991.
b Give reasons to explain the pattern of change.
c Draw a pie chart to show the places of birth for Small Heath's population.
d What does this information tell you about the people who have made the area grow?

5 Study Source G. Calculate the percentage of people who own their home.

6 *The Government are assessing the success of Small Health as a 'General Improvement Area'. You have been invited to respond using the headings: • value for money, • improving the environment, • retaining a sense of community.*

9·4 Castle Vale: residents plan changes

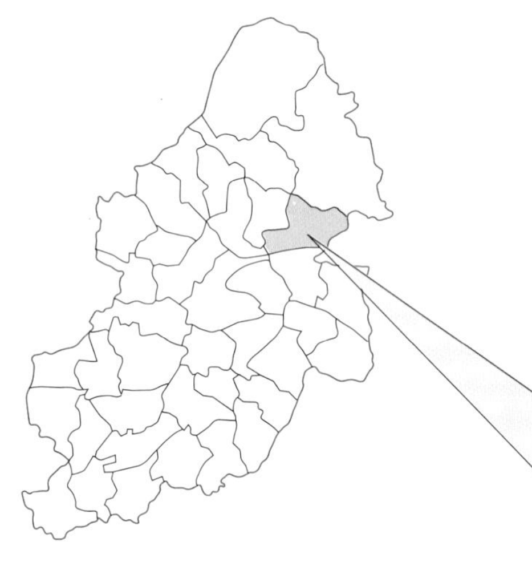

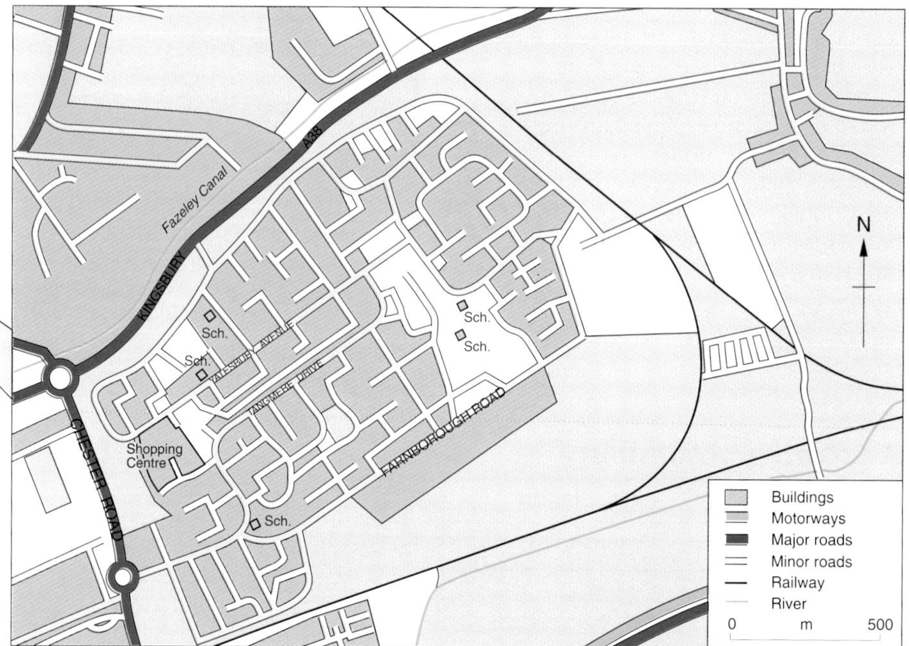

Source A Castle Vale estate, Kingsbury Ward

Redeveloping the urban fringe

In March 1993, residents of Castle Vale voted to take responsibility for their own future. People living in the flats, maisonettes and houses supported the creation of a Housing Action Trust, run by a local board of managers. The Trust will be responsible for the 250-hectare estate and a 130 million programme of improvements agreed between the City Council and the Government. The project will:

- install central heating into maisonettes and flats
- redevelop the shopping and community centres
- provide a safer road network
- extend the crime prevention programme.

Eight tower blocks will be demolished and residents' own ideas on housing will replace the ideas of the 1960s' planners.

Source B Castle Vale from the air

Source C The entrance to the estate

1 a Use Sources A and B to draw a fully labelled sketch map of the area. Include on your map:

- such features as the roads and railway lines which form a boundary to the estate
- the shopping centre and the car park
- areas of tower blocks and low-rise housing
- schools, churches and playing fields.

Give your map a title and key.

b Describe the HOUSING DENSITY of this area.

Why we love the Vale

Source D The shopping centre, soon to be refurbished by the Housing Action Trust

There's a pride in the Vale that I didn't expect when I came here. It isn't as bad as people make out. The problem is that, although there are facilities for the very young and the old, there is nothing for teenagers, who get bored and cause trouble. The bus runs every ten minutes to the city centre, but it does take half an hour.

Source E Gary Smith

I have lived on the Vale for 24 years. Although my flat was broken into last week for the second time, I couldn't live anywhere else. For pensioners it is the best place in the world. It offers you everything. I'm on the committee of the social club, play bingo three times a week and everyone knows me at the local shops and church.

Source F Mr Aggarwal

Source G Improved housing

Source H Castle Vale Neighbourhood Office

There is a great deal of hardship for some people living on the estate. But, among the large number of single parents, there are some who are trying hard to make a better life for themselves. I often see them when they leave their children at the crèche to attend adult education classes provided by the comprehensive school. These busy mums don't use the swimming pool very much and they never allow their children to use the playgrounds around the flats.

Source I Ailin Christie, community worker

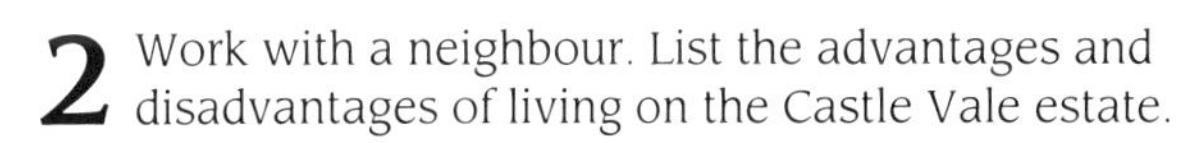

2 Work with a neighbour. List the advantages and disadvantages of living on the Castle Vale estate.

3 Make a large copy of the table below:

Indicator	Measuring environmental quality						
	C	D	E	F	G	H	I
Attractiveness							
Litter							
Leisure services							
Graffiti							
Friendliness							

a For each source, grade the environment: good (3), average (2) or poor (1), for the five indicators. You might not be able to comment on every indicator for each source.
b Add two further indicators of your own and grade them.
c *This table is called an* ENVIRONMENTAL QUALITY MATRIX. *What does it tell you about the quality of the Castle Vale environment? Do you think it is a fair test? Explain why.*

9·5 Four Oaks Park . . .

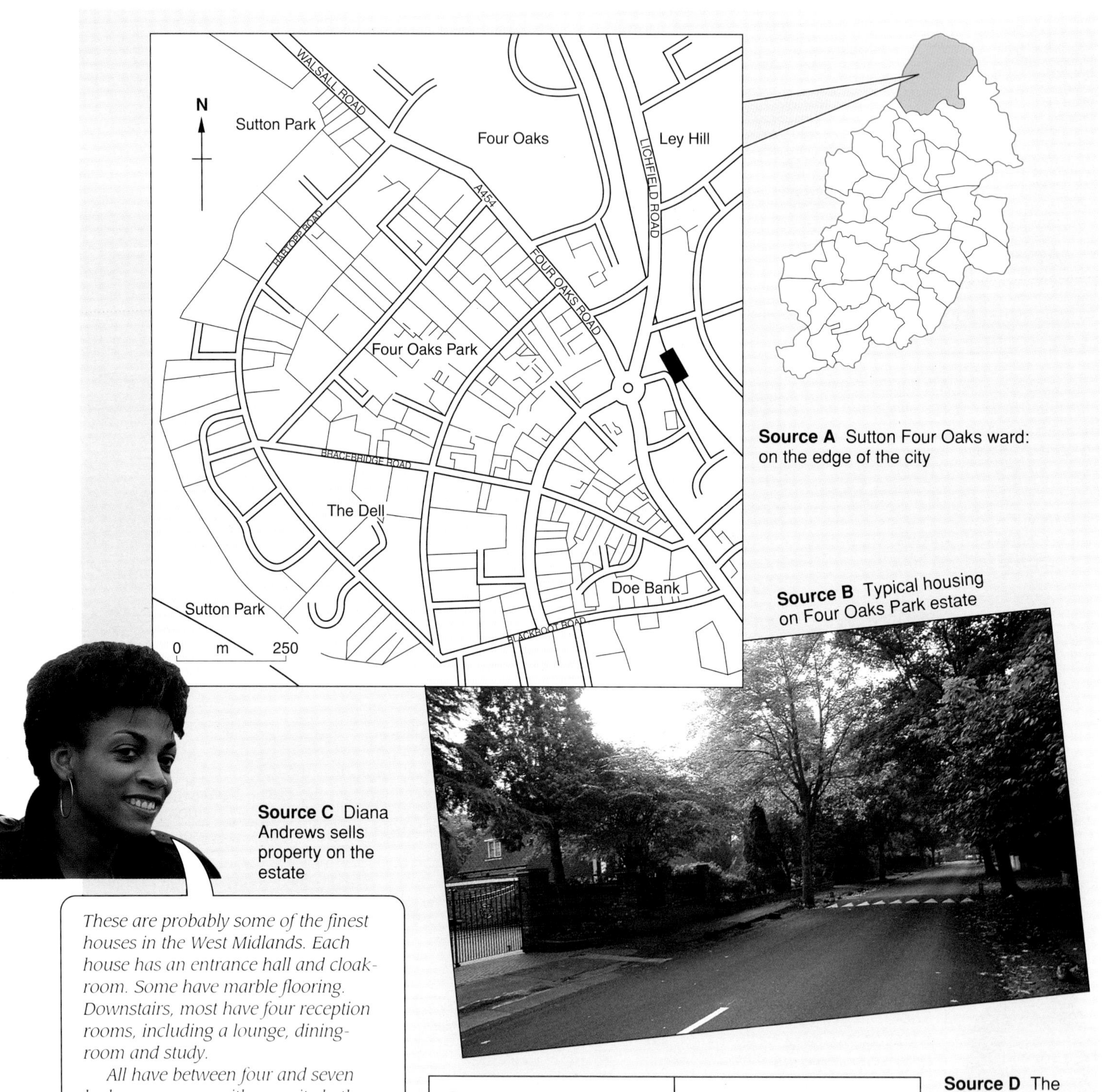

Source A Sutton Four Oaks ward: on the edge of the city

Source B Typical housing on Four Oaks Park estate

Source C Diana Andrews sells property on the estate

These are probably some of the finest houses in the West Midlands. Each house has an entrance hall and cloak-room. Some have marble flooring. Downstairs, most have four reception rooms, including a lounge, dining-room and study.

All have between four and seven bedrooms, some with en-suite bath-rooms with sunken jacuzzi baths. Most have sauna and shower rooms.

Gardens are massive, secluded and well-maintained, and there is a range of indoor and outdoor swimming pools on the estate. Double garages are standard.

The cheapest house	The most expensive house
Purchase price: £195 000	Purchase price: £695 000
Down payment: £39 000	Down payment: £139 000
Monthly payments: £975	Monthly payments: £3 475

Source D The cost of a mortgage for houses on the Four Oaks Park estate, 1993

. . . but only for a few

1 Study Sources A and B.
a Describe the location and environment of Four Oaks Park estate.
b Describe the pattern of housing on the Four Oaks Park estate. Comment on how the road pattern affects the size the plots.
c Why might this estate be described as 'exclusive'?

2 Study Sources A, B and C. Using either an environmental quality matrix or a copy of the diagram on page 61, assess the quality of the Four Oaks Park environment.

3 Produce an estate agent's brochure for a house on the Four Oaks estate. You should include a labelled plan of the house as well as a written description.

Who lives on the estate?

Source E This resident has lived on the estate for twelve years

Peace and privacy are very important to me. As the Chief Executive of a Birmingham-based multi-national company, I travel all over the world. Birmingham International airport has a good shuttle service to London Heathrow, where I fly to our offices in Berlin, Tokyo, Sydney and New York. But, I do like coming home. I enjoy relaxing by the pool, playing a round of golf, or just nipping down the road to the tennis club.

The population of Sutton Four Oaks

Households with:	Percentage
No car	17
1 car	38
2 cars	36
3+ cars	9

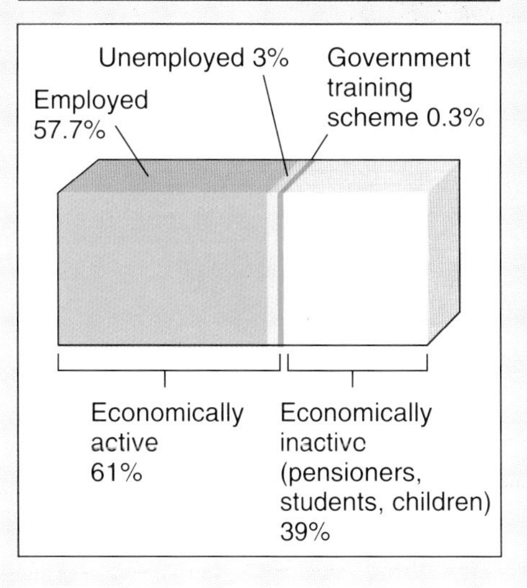

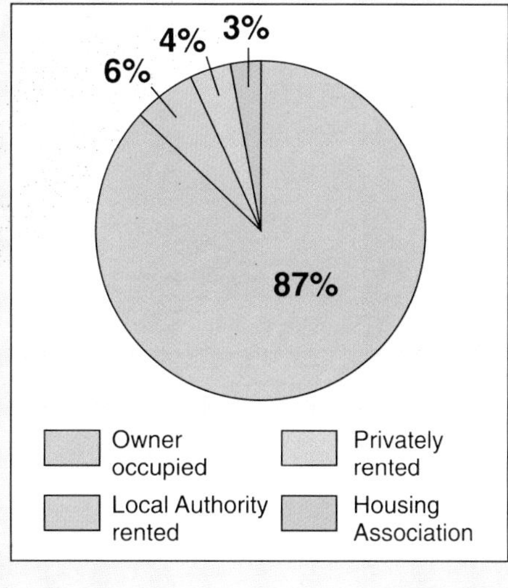

Source F Census data, Four Oaks ward, 1991

Ethnic origin	Percentage
White	97
Black Caribbean	0.1
Indian	1.2
Chinese	0.1
Other Asian	0.1
Irish	1.3
Other	0.2

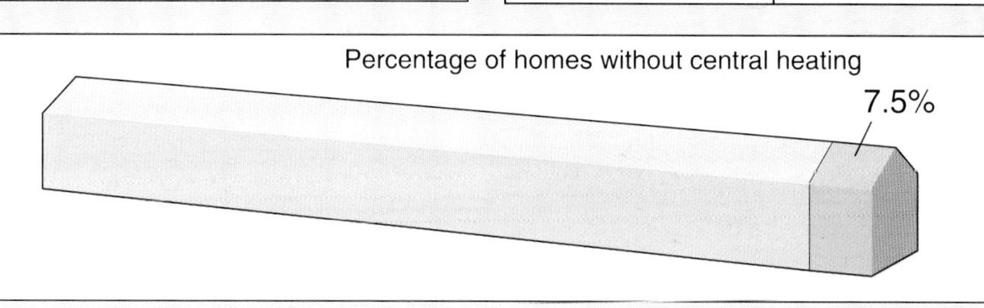

4 Study Source D. Banks and building societies will lend around three times a person's salary for a MORTGAGE.
a How much would a person need to earn each year to pay the mortgage on: • the cheapest property, • the most expensive property?
b With a partner discuss the possible occupations of the residents who can afford the prices of this estate.

5 Study Sources B and E. Explain how and why people living on Four Oaks Park estate might wish to protect their privacy.

6 Study Source F.
a Write a description of a 'typical' family living in Four Oaks.
b Suggest why such a description might be misleading.
c Suggest why there is little population movement in this area.

7 *Using the information on pages 58–67, compare and contrast the residents of Four Oaks with residents of other areas of Birmingham.*

9·6 Getting a fair deal

Positive action

People in Birmingham benefit from growing up in multi-cultural communities. The City Council has a strong commitment to equal opportunities, especially in education, housing and employment. Nonetheless, there are many difficulties that people still have to overcome.

Source A Birmingham: multi-cultural communities have many strengths but also face many challenges

We want to improve our homes. In this area the City Council is slow to repair houses and pay grants for renovations. Poor housing makes our living conditions difficult. Our homes become less valuable and harder to sell. We know that things are different in other parts of the inner city. We pay our taxes. We deserve a fair share of the benefits.

Text adapted from the *Express and Star*, 13 October 1992

Source B Facing the difficulties

Source C A teacher helps a cycle of success

1 Study Source A.
a Describe the scene shown in the photograph.
b With a partner, make a list of the challenges that the people might face.
c Make a second list of the rights that they have.

2 Study Source B.
a About what problem are the men protesting?
b Suggest reasons why they are protesting.
c What would you do if you had been treated unfairly in a shop or at school? Explain your answer.

3 Study Source C.
a In pairs, discuss what you understand by the term 'positive role model'. Why might the teacher be described in this manner?
b Who would you consider as a positive role model for yourself? Explain why.

4 Use Sources B and C.
a Describe how positive action can create a cycle of success.
b What might be a starting point to the circle? Explain why.
c With a partner, discuss how the cycle might be broken.

Unemployment in Birmingham

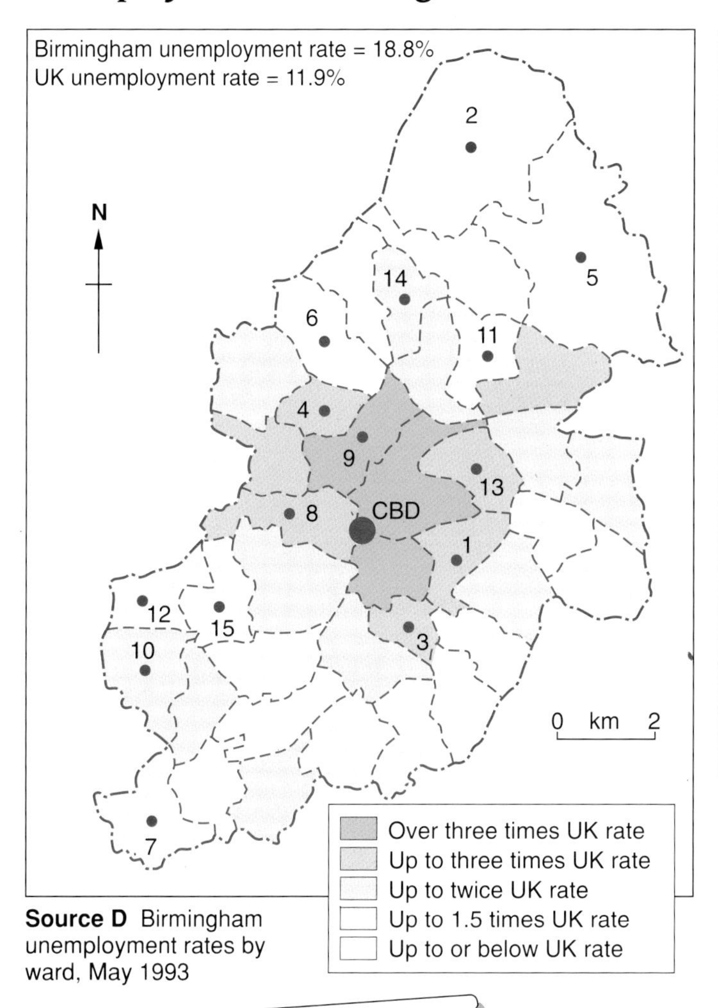

Source D Birmingham unemployment rates by ward, May 1993

Ward	No. on map	Population (%)		
		Afro-Caribbean	Asian	Irish
Small Heath	1	7	41	6.5
Sutton Four Oaks	2	0	1	2
Sparkhill	3	7	43	7
Handsworth	4	22	31	5
Sutton New Hall	5	0.7	1	3
Perry Barr	6	5	3	4
Longbridge	7	2	0.6	4
Ladywood	8	15	17	7
Aston	9	19	25	7
Bartley Green	10	2.5	1	3
Erdington	11	3	2	8
Quinton	12	2	3	4
Washwood Heath	13	5	23	5
Kingstanding	14	3	1	5
Harborne	15	2	3	4
Birmingham average		5.2	10.3	5

Source E Ethnic minority populations of selected wards, May 1993

WHITE SUPPORT ESSENTIAL

Last week, the Indian Workers Association criticised Britain's white trade unionists for not doing enough to fight racism.

RACIAL HARMONY CONTRACT

Council tenants who are buying their homes will have to sign a contract promising not to racially harass or abuse their neighbours.

Birmingham City Council
Open Access to Jobs

As the largest employer in the City, with over 50,000 employees, we have regular vacancies at all levels. We particularly welcome applications from black and minority ethnic people who are under-represented in our workforce.

BLACK UNEMPLOYMENT ON THE INCREASE

... Researchers claimed that more than 50 per cent of employers discriminated against black applicants for jobs.

Equal Opportunities Commission raps banks for not employing enough black staff and for not promoting women.

Source F Positive initiatives

5 Using Sources D and E:

a Draw a graph to show unemployment against distance from the CBD. (Measure from the mid-point of the CBD to the mid-point of each ward.)
b Describe the relationship shown by your graph.
c Draw a second graph to show the ethnic minority populations of each ward. You could draw the graph on tracing paper so that it can be placed over your first graph.
d Describe the relationships between unemployment and the size of ethnic minority populations.

6 Study Source F.

a List ideas about making Birmingham a better place for the people in Source A. Suggest reasons for your choice.
b Describe the evidence which shows that ethnic minority populations have been unfairly treated by many employers.
c Suggest ways in which employment opportunities can be improved for members of ethnic minorities.
d Use your answer to **2c** to help suggest how people feel about discrimination by employers.
e Using the sources and your own experiences, identify other groups of people who suffer discrimination.

7 The City Council has asked for advice about dealing with prejudice and discrimination. Choose one of the following:
• housing, • education, • employment.
a In a small group, discuss what advice should be given.
b *Produce a short written report.*

9·7 Birmingham: visions of the future

Future development depends on selling Birmingham as a rich and lively city, as well as attracting business and industry. The city has to lose its Victorian image and repair the damage caused by motorway construction and the architecture of the 1960s.

Newtown City Challenge bid

In April 1992, Birmingham's bid for the Government's City Challenge fund was successful and the city won £37.5 million for a five-year regeneration programme. The proposal was based upon two areas, the Newtown Shopping Centre and the former Lucas Industries' factory in Aston.

In 1960, Newtown had a population of 35 000 people. By the 1990s, clearance and depopulation had left a deprived area where figures for crime, poverty, ill-health and unemployment were high. The aim was to improve education and create job opportunities. In April 1993 work began to develop 40 hectares of land for business and industry, and housing and community use.

Source A Taking up the city challenge

The Lucas Industries site, Aston

Five years from now Newtown South Aston will be on the way to being busier, cleaner, safer, more prosperous, healthier and more firmly linked to the rest of the City Centre. Its education and training services will be a model for the inner-city areas to follow and its ugly and blighted vacant sites will have disappeared. Increasingly the local community, including its business and voluntary sector, will be organised and running itself.

City Challenge 1992 Newtown South Aston

Source B Success in the city

1 Study Sources A and B.
a Using one of the methods described on pages 61 and 65, assess the environmental quality of the City Challenge area.
b Suggest ways in which the environmental quality of the area might be improved.

2 Study Sources C, D, E and F. In pairs:
a List the improvements made to the city centre.
b Make a list of other improvements that might be made.
c Under each of the five priorities for developing the city, identify how the improvements listed in **a** and **b** might benefit the city.

3 Study Source G.
a Where are most of the regeneration areas situated?
b What do you think is meant by 'partnership core area'?
c Choose three development areas in Birmingham and, using information in this unit, describe:
• why the areas were chosen for redevelopment
• what is being done to improve the area.

4 Using this unit:
a Describe the history and impact of urban renewal throughout Birmingham under the headings: • new homes, • the movement of people, • other facilities.
b Which people seem to have been least effected by all the changes?
c Suggest how the history of urban renewal may influence future patterns of housing in the city.

City centre revival

Source C The Birmingham Repertory and the International Conference Centre

Source D Centenary Square

Source E PEDESTRIANISATION of New Street

In 1993, Birmingham City Council produced an action plan for urban regeneration. Called 'A Force for Change', it identifies targets and areas for development. It aims to change people's image of Birmingham. The plan has five priorities:

- to encourage local investment
- to bring outside investment into the city
- to reduce the loss of industry from the city
- to limit the effects of disadvantages
- to promote local business and residents to the UK Government, the European Community and on the international scene.

Source F Paradise Circus

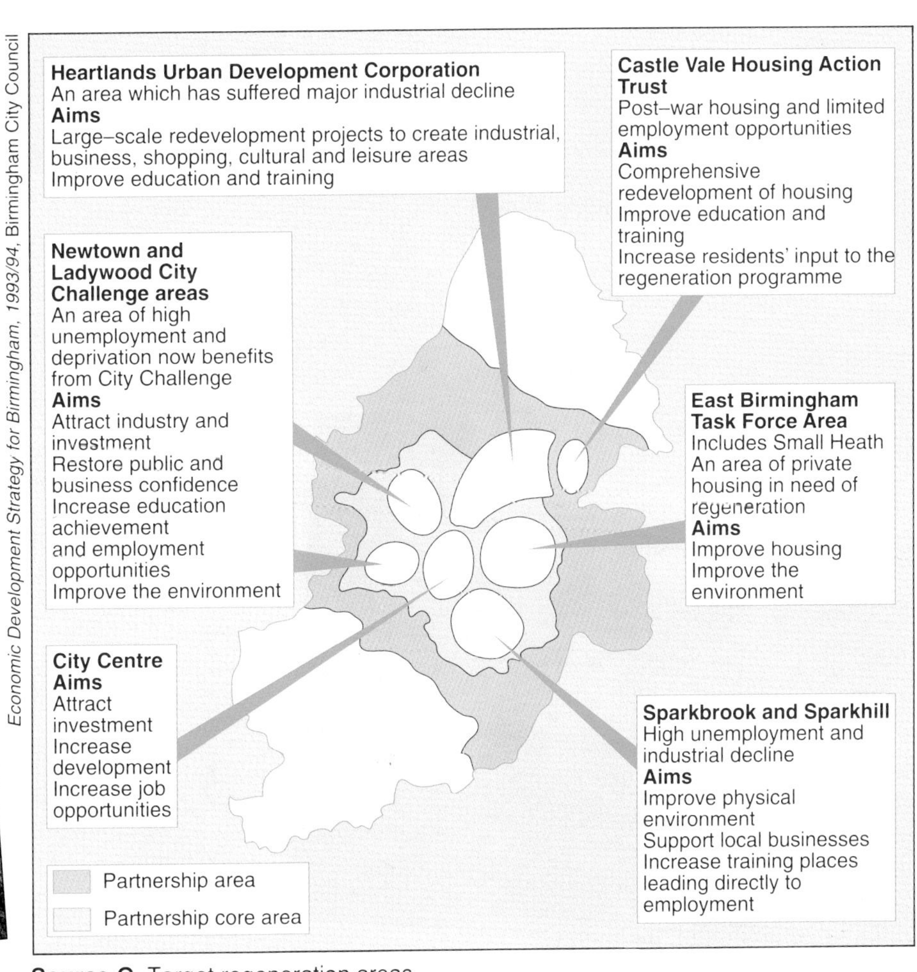

Heartlands Urban Development Corporation
An area which has suffered major industrial decline
Aims
Large-scale redevelopment projects to create industrial, business, shopping, cultural and leisure areas
Improve education and training
Castle Vale Housing Action Trust
Post-war housing and limited employment opportunities
Aims
Comprehensive redevelopment of housing
Improve education and training
Increase residents' input to the regeneration programme
Newtown and Ladywood City Challenge areas
An area of high unemployment and deprivation now benefits from City Challenge
Aims
Attract industry and investment
Restore public and business confidence
Increase education achievement and employment opportunities
Improve the environment
East Birmingham Task Force Area
Includes Small Heath
An area of private housing in need of regeneration
Aims
Improve housing
Improve the environment
City Centre
Aims
Attract investment
Increase development
Increase job opportunities
Sparkbrook and Sparkhill
High unemployment and industrial decline
Aims
Improve physical environment
Support local businesses
Increase training places leading directly to employment
Partnership area
Partnership core area

Economic Development Strategy for Birmingham, 1993/94, Birmingham City Council

Source G Target regeneration areas

10·1 PLANNING ROAD IMPROVEMENTS

Road traffic in the UK is increasing. Some people want more and wider roads. However, building new roads in the countryside is always controversial: roads may improve accessibility, but they bring environmental costs. Who benefits from new roads and who loses? How are planning decisions made?

Problems in the Pennines

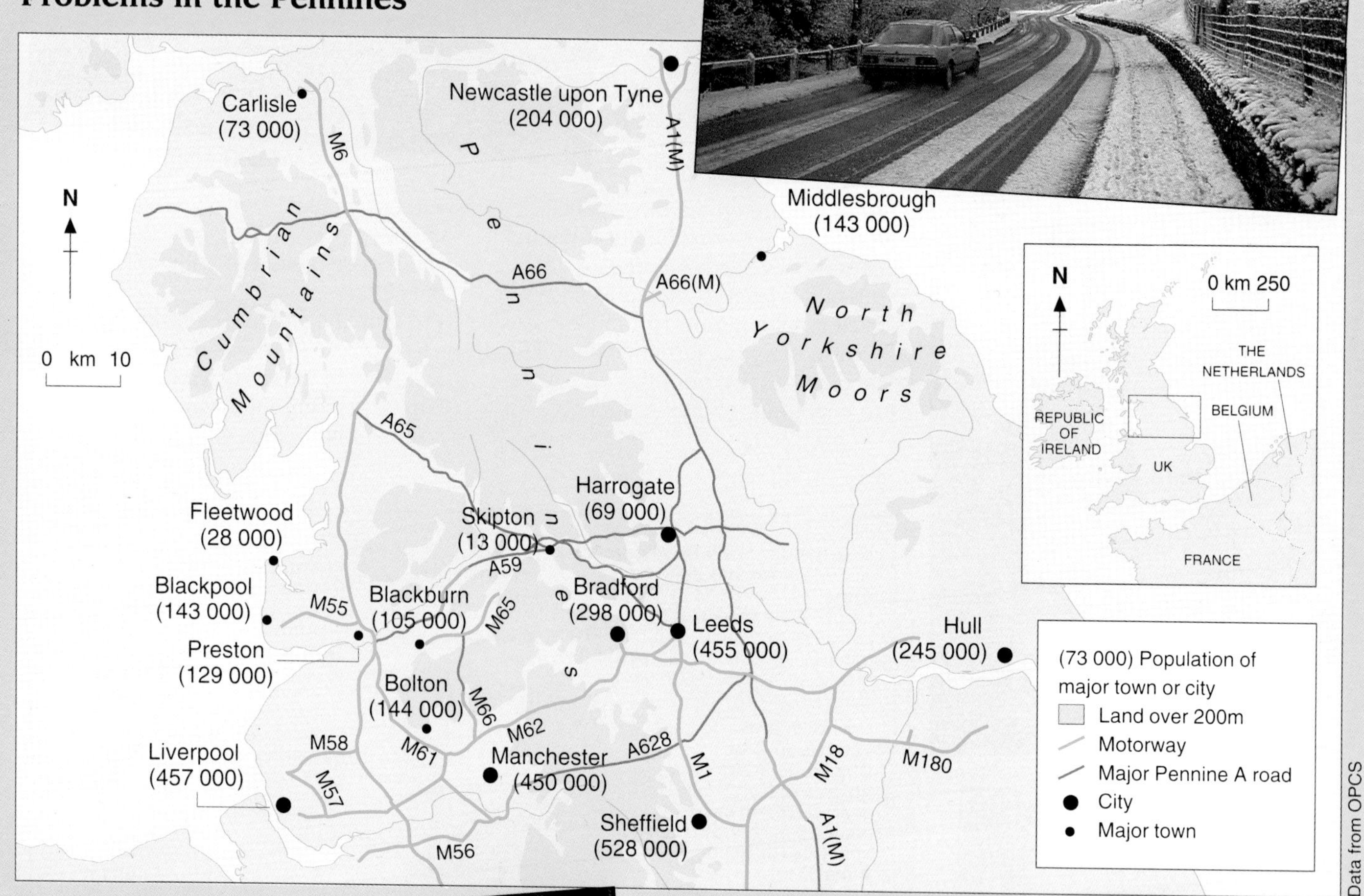

Source A A North Yorkshire road in winter

Source C Northern England: major cross-Pennine road links

Source B Holiday traffic on the A65

1 a Study Sources A and B. Describe each environment.
b What problems for cross-Pennine travel are suggested here?

2 Using Source C:
a Describe the location of the Pennines within England.
b Suggest why there are few major cross-Pennine road routes.

3 Using Source C:
a Describe the shortest routes both by road and motorway between: • Sheffield and Manchester, • Leeds and Carlisle.
b Why might it sometimes be quicker to take a longer route for each of the two journeys?
c Explain why you think there are not more major road or motorway links across the Pennines.

Why are new and better roads needed?

Nationally

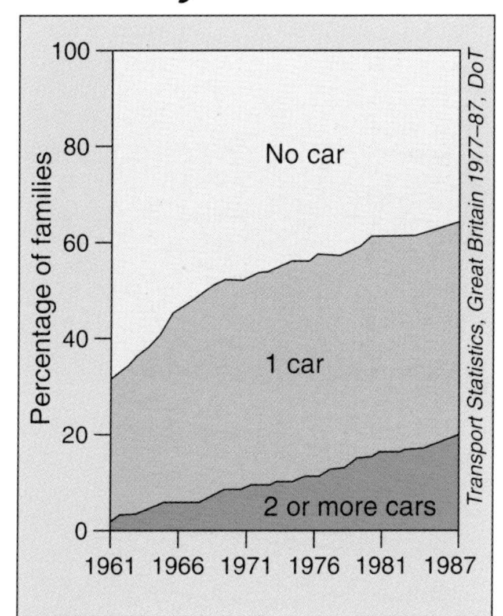

Source D Car ownership in Britain, 1961–87

Year	Number of passenger kilometres (billions) by type of transport			
1962	152	65	37	1.1
1972	325	51	35	2.2
1982	421	41	31	2.9
1989	563	41	40	4.9

Transport and the Environment, DoT, 1991

Source E Types of passenger transport, 1962–89, UK

Year	Domestic freight transport (in billion tonne/km)				
	Road	**Rail**	**Water**	**Pipeline**	**Total**
1979	102	20	56	10	188
1989	137	17	58	9	221

Transport and the Environment, DoT, 1991

Source F Transporting domestic freight, UK

4 **a** Explain what Source D tells you about car ownership in Britain.
b Study Source E. Draw a line graph to show the trend in preferred types of passenger transport since 1962.
c Study Source F. How much of the 33 billion tonne increase in freight movement has been taken by road transport? Explain your answer.

5 What do Sources D, E and F suggest about the need for new roads? Explain your answer.

Across the Pennines

Source G Traffic on the A629, Keighley

- Many major A roads go through small towns and villages, causing much congestion and slowing down travel.
- Cross-Pennine traffic is expected to increase by up to 78 per cent by the year 2011, and 92 per cent by 2016.
- It is expected that the importance of a direct link from Europe to Ireland, through Hull and Fleetwood (Source C), will grow over the next ten years.

Route	Maximum altitude (metres)
1 Widening the M62 to four lanes in each direction	400
2 Upgrading the A65/A59 to link with the M65	200
3 Upgrading the A628 to dual carriageway	500
4 Upgrading the A66 to dual carriageway	550
5 Building a new road close to the A59 from Harrogate to Skipton	300

Source H Cross-Pennine route suggestions

6 Using Sources A, C and H:
a Locate where each proposed route goes.
b Explain why the maximum altitude of a proposed route is important to the PLANNERS.

7 *a Work with a partner. With the information available, decide which route would be most useful for linking built-up areas.*
b Write a brief report to explain your choice and list other information you think should be considered before a decision is made.

10·2 An improved cross-Pennine route

One possible route for much of the increased cross-Pennine traffic is the A65/A59. In recent years, a number of improvements have been made to the route. BY-PASSES have been built round towns and villages providing an alternative road for through traffic. Sections of existing road have been upgraded to dual carriageway.

The section from Otley to Skipton runs along Wharfedale. The only major settlement yet to be by-passed is Ilkley. The Department of Transport feels that an Ilkley by-pass should be built soon.

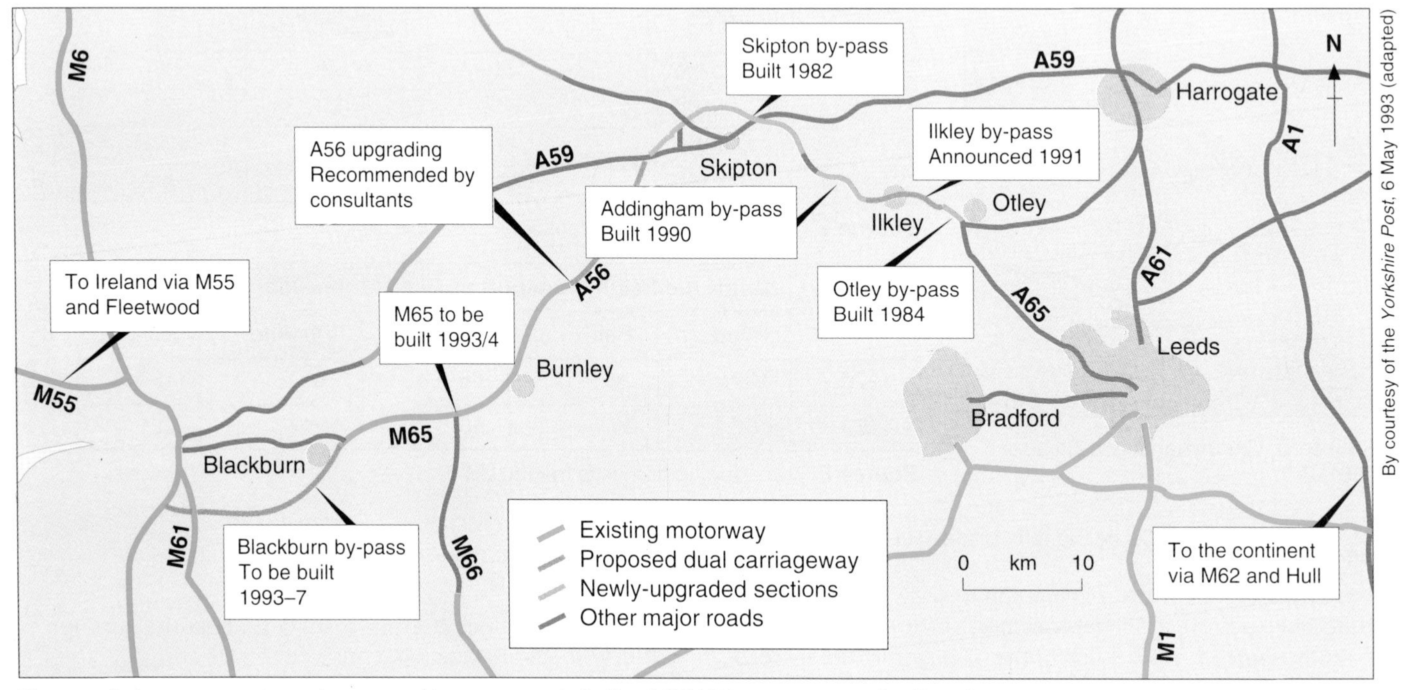

By courtesy of the *Yorkshire Post*, 6 May 1993 (adapted)

Source A Improvements and proposed improvements to the A65/A59 route across the Pennines

Why provide a by-pass?

The A65 trunk road which passes through the main commercial and residential areas of Ilkley, is part of the road network linking Leeds with the M6 and the Lake District.
The route through Ilkley cannot accommodate large amounts of traffic, particularly lorries. Narrow roads and footpaths add to the difficulties.
The traffic also carries a severe environmental impact on the Ilkley conservation area. About half of the traffic is 'through traffic' which could use a bypass.
The accident rate in the town is twice that which could be expected for this type of road.
Unless the problem is addressed now, conditions will become intolerable.

A65 Ilkley Bypass Public Consultation, DoT

Source C Traffic in Ilkley town centre

Source D A view of upper Wharfedale

The Ilkley by-pass

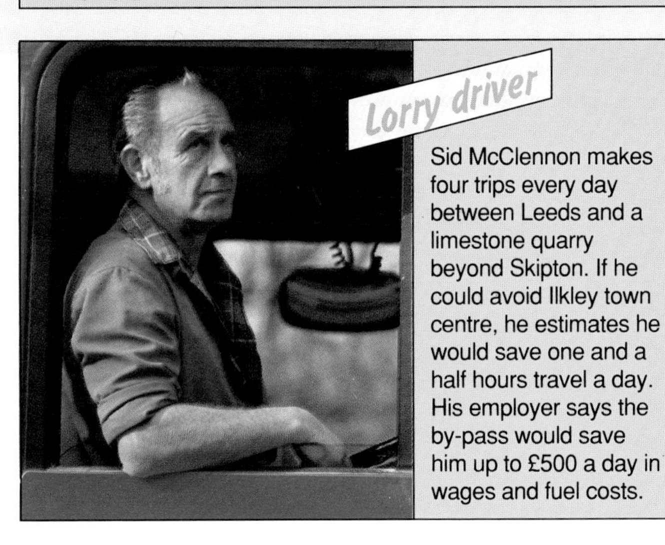

The Benson family live in Leeds. They are keen caravanners and regularly drive through Ilkley on their way to the Lake District. They have calculated that an Ilkley by-pass will cut 35–45 minutes from their journey.

Sid McClennon makes four trips every day between Leeds and a limestone quarry beyond Skipton. If he could avoid Ilkley town centre, he estimates he would save one and a half hours travel a day. His employer says the by-pass would save him up to £500 a day in wages and fuel costs.

Tim Zillessen commutes to Leeds through Ilkley. He estimates that the by-pass will reduce his journey by ten minutes a day.

Source B Views of local road users

1 **a** Using Source A, describe the journey you would make from Otley to the M6. Mention which sections of the route have recently been improved and how, and which sections have yet to be improved.
b When all the improvements are complete, the road will not be of the same width or standard. What problems might this cause traffic?

2 Study Source B. Which two road users have the same reason for wanting to see a by-pass for Ilkley? Explain why.

3 Use an atlas to help you. On a journey to Carlisle, would you use the proposed Ilkley by-pass if you were travelling from:
- Bristol, • Birmingham, • London, • Derby, • Norwich,
- Oxford?

Improved accessibility

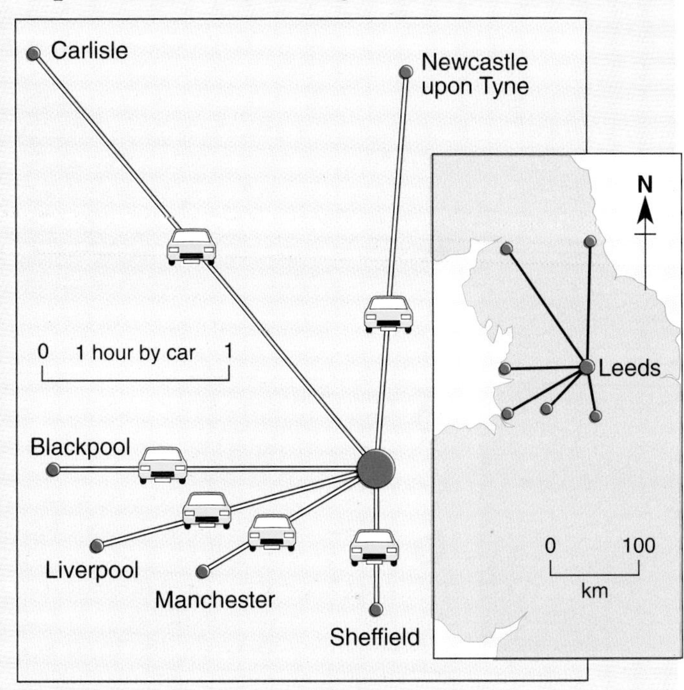

Source E Time–distance map of car journeys from Leeds

A new road by-passing the Pennine towns and villages would reduce current journey times, but it is not clear by how much. However, it is clear that Leeds would be more ACCESSIBLE from the West.

4 Study Source C. Suggest, in your own words, the three reasons given by the Department of Transport for Ilkley needing a by-pass.

5 Study Sources C and D.
a Describe the scenery of upper Wharfedale.
b What other advantages might there be for Ilkley in having a by-pass?
c Suggest disadvantages there might be for the people of Ilkley.

6 Study Source E.
a List the current journey times by car from Leeds to each destination.
b Which journeys would not be affected by the building of the Ilkley by-pass?
c Make a copy of Source E to show a 20 minute saving in journey times resulting from the building of the Ilkley by-pass.

7 *How can the advantages of a shorter journey be compared with the effects on the environment of building a by-pass?*

10·3 Effects on the environment

Not everyone sees the Ilkley by-pass as an improvement for the area. The Chairman of the Wharfedale Access Group says: 'They can always make more cars, they can always make more roads, but no one can ever build another Wharfedale. It is a priceless landscape and we must do everything in our power to protect it.' Other residents of the area feel the same.

Farmer

John Fryer farms 49 hectares in the Wharfe Valley. If the by-pass goes ahead, much of this land will be buried under tarmac and his farm will be cut in two by a four-lane highway. 'I will have to reduce the size of my herd of cows and this might put my farm out of business.'

Rambler

Ann Bickley has walked hundreds of kilometres on the paths around Ilkley. If the road goes ahead, twelve of these paths will be cut in two. 'The view of Ilkley from the Cow and Calf Rocks will be changed for ever, and the tranquillity beyond Middleton will have been lost.'

Nature lover

Catherine Lister has lived in Nesfield all her life. 'If the by-pass is built, a flyover will be necessary just below Nesfield. Trees will be felled and concrete piles sunk. I wonder where we are heading with all these roads.'

Source A Worried local residents

Can good road design conserve the environment?

A69 Cumbria: viaducts allow property and other historical features to be saved

M6 Cumbria: the impact of the road is absorbed by the scale of the hills around

A well-designed badger crossing

Source C Environmental considerations in road design

The Department of Transport say they are concerned about nature conservation and damage to the rural landscape. 'The Good Roads Guide' gives examples of environmental issues which they consider when designing roads.

5 Study Sources A and C. Explain to what extent the concerns of the local residents could be answered by good road design.

6 **a** What would need to be done in order to protect:

- wild deer straying on to a major road
- a piece of ancient woodland?

b What other features of the environment might need protecting? Work with a partner to suggest possible solutions.

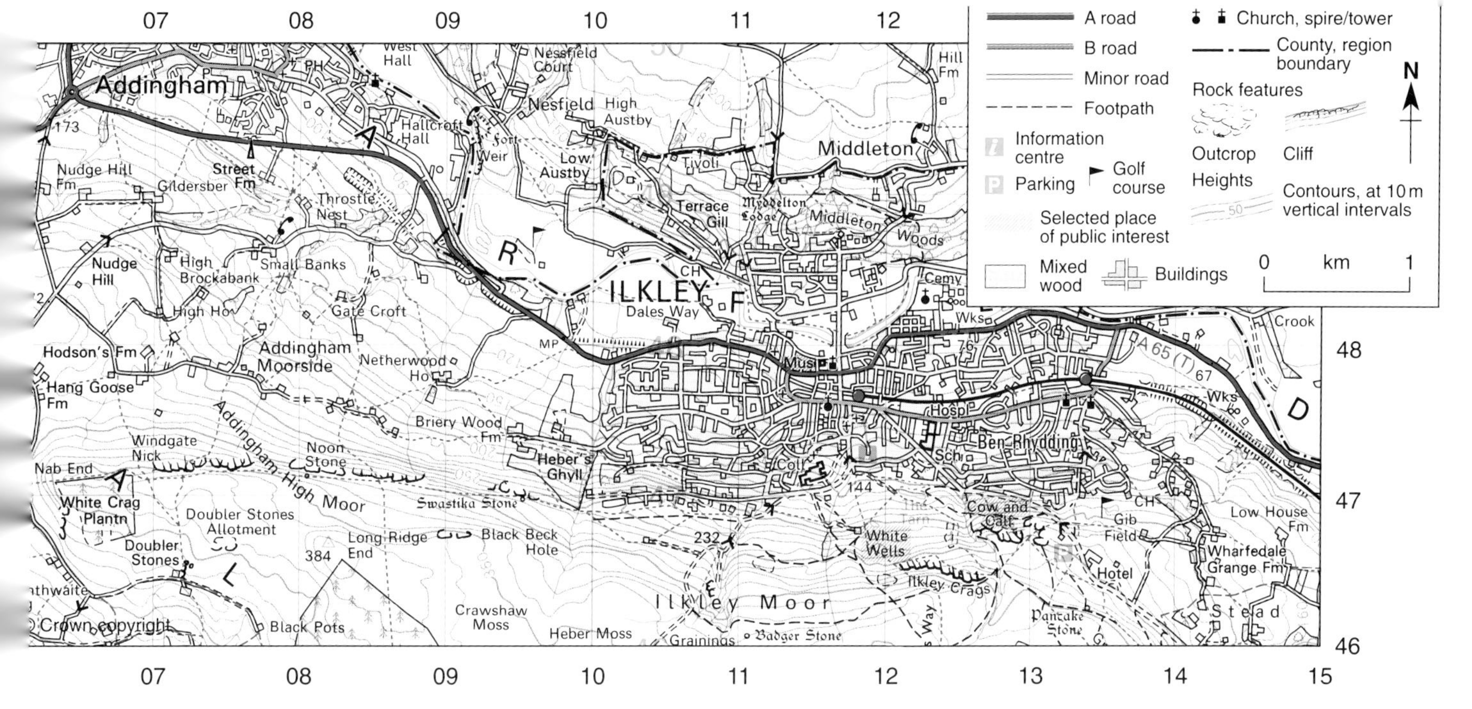

Source B Ordnance Survey map of the Ilkley area

1 a Study Source A. Explain why these three local residents are against the by-pass.
b Work with a partner. Compare the reasons given by the three residents with the three road users on page 75. Decide who puts forward the most persuasive view. Explain why.

2 a Draw a sketch map from Source B. Make it A4 in size. On it mark:
- the Cow and Calf Rocks and Nesfield
- the built-up area of Ilkley
- the A65 road
- woodland areas
- the River Wharfe
- the two ends of the proposed by-pass at GR 089489 and 139481.

Give your map a title and add a key.

3 Using Source B:
a Which side of the valley has the steepest slopes?
b Describe the relationship between relief and slope, and relief and the major lines of communication.
c Describe the location of Ilkley in relation to the River Wharfe Valley.

4 The routes for the proposed by-pass all go to the north of the town. What reasons can you find on Source B which suggest why the south of the town does not offer suitable routes?

New roads bring other changes

At Addingham, near Ilkley, more than 24 hectares of farmland and open space between the village and the new ring road have been proposed for housing, recreation and industrial development by Bradford Council.

7 The development shown in Source D is called 'creeping URBANISATION'. Explain what you think this means.

8 a Using Sources B and D, draw a sketch map of Addingham at a scale of 1:25 000 (double the scale of the Ordnance Survey map, Source B). On it mark:
- the by-pass
- the extent of the built-up area
- the River Wharfe
- the areas of proposed housing and commercial development.

Give your map a title and a key.
b With a partner, discuss advantages and disadvantages of the proposed by-pass for Addingham.

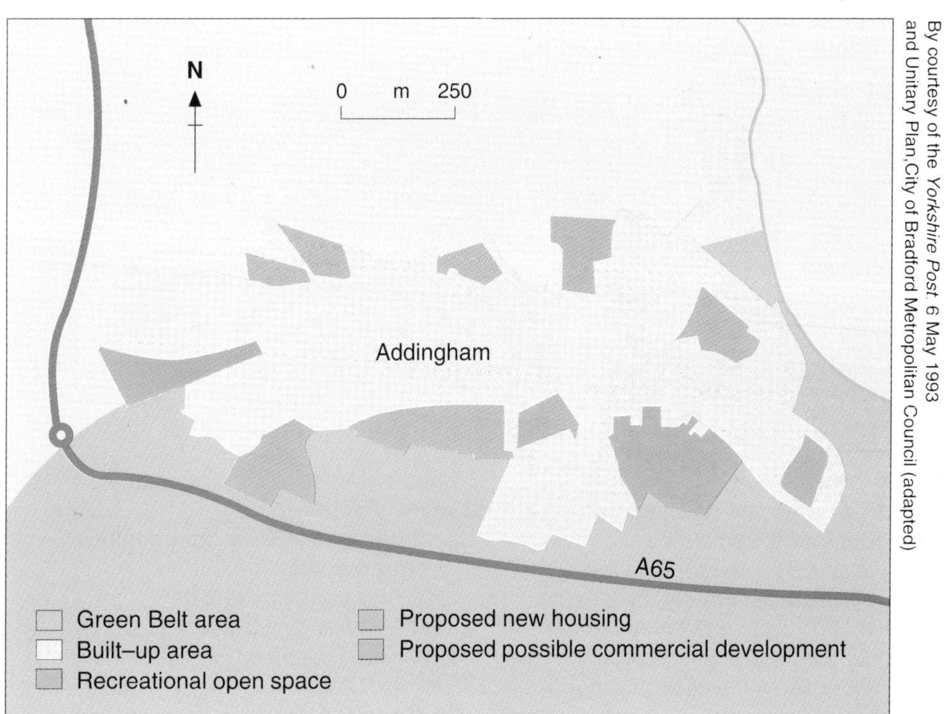

Source D Land use development plan for Addingham

By courtesy of the *Yorkshire Post* 6 May 1993 and Unitary Plan, City of Bradford Metropolitan Council (adapted)

10·4 Which route? Who decides?

Four routes for public discussion

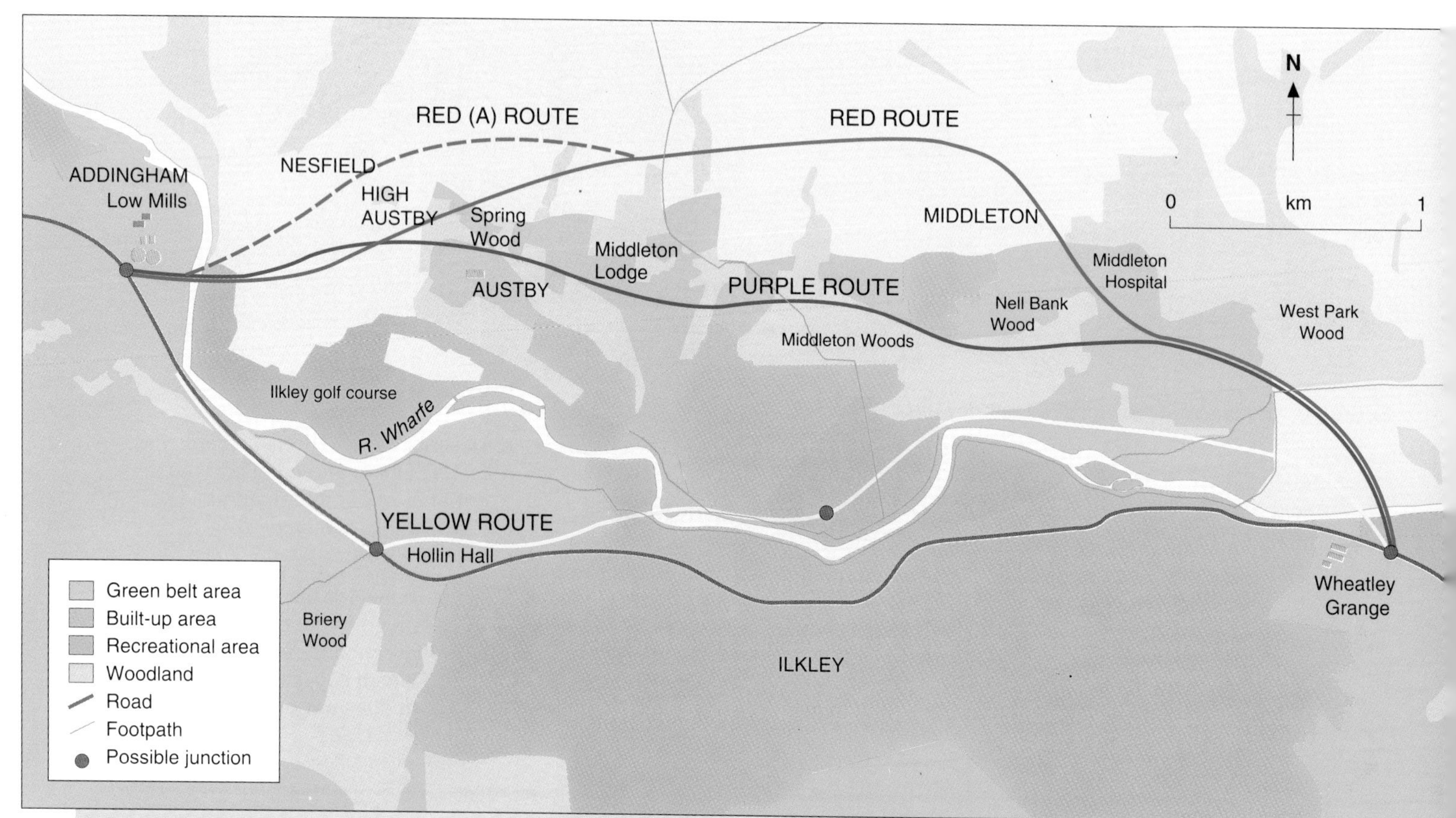

Source A The Department of Transport has proposed four routes for the Ilkley by-pass

Route	Length (km)	Advantages	Disadvantages	Area of land required (hectares)	Estimated cost (£ million)
Red	5.8	No demolition of property Less visible from the town Avoids main woodlands	Takes more farmland than the the purple or yellow routes	29–33	11–17
Red (A)		No demolition of property	Takes the most farmland	29–33	11–17
Purple				26–30	10–15
Yellow		Removes the most traffic from existing roads Takes the least farmland Less steep gradients	Passes close to communities	20–21	14–16

Source B Comparison of routes

1 Study Sources A and B.
a Make a copy of Source B. Leave about four lines below each route to give space for the tasks below.
b Measure accurately the lengths of the Red (A), Purple and Yellow routes and write the answers in your table.
c Place the phrases below in the correct boxes under the 'Advantages' and 'Disadvantages' columns:
- the shortest route
- furthest away from communities
- requires most demolition
- avoids main woodlands
- the lowest construction cost
- the greatest effect on recreation and leisure facilities
- steeper gradients.

2 The Yellow route is as expensive as the others, although it uses less land. Why is this so?

3 The Red (A) route is only slightly different from the Red Route. Describe the difference and suggest why this route has been proposed.

The planning process

1. Investigation of routes
2. Public consultation of routes
3. Preferred route announced
4. Further investigation of preferred route and draft decision published
5. Possible public inquiry
6. Final decision after consideration of objections
7. Land bought and construction started

A town centre craftshop owner who relies on the tourist trade
A resident of Middleton Close who uses Ilkley for all his shopping
The farmer at High Austby who has a mixed herd of sheep and cows
A haulage contractor whose firm is based near the centre of Ilkley

Source D At the public consultation, four residents of the Ilkley area put forward their views about the proposed routes

Source C The decision-making process in planning a new road is very lengthy. Ten years is not a long time to get from stage 1 to stage 7

4 Study Source C. What are the two stages at which local people and interest groups can put their ideas forward?

5 Work in a group of four:
- Choose one of the roles described in Source D.
- Use Sources A and B, to decide which by-pass route would suit you and why.
- Explain your decision and reasons to the rest of the group.

Stop press: decision made!

PRESS NOTICE

THE DEPARTMENT OF TRANSPORT

Press Notice No: YH/481/92
Date: 17 December 1992

Preferred route for Ilkley Bypass

Improved safety on the A65 in Wharfedale, West Yorkshire, came closer today.
Kenneth Carlisle, Minister for Roads and Traffic, today announced that the preferred route for the Ilkley Bypass is the most northerly of the four routes put forward at Public Consultation.
The chosen route, Red (A), has been amended at its eastern end to pass through the site of the disused Middleton Hospital.

Source E Press notice of the draft decision

6 Study Source E. How pleased is each person in Source D likely to be with this decision? Explain why.

7 *Study pages 72, 73 and 74. In the light of the decision on a route for the Ilkley by-pass, do you think the A59/65 will develop into a major cross-Pennine route? Explain your opinion.*

11·1 MASS TRANSPORT IN JAPAN

Many people travel daily into cities. Why is this? What problems are caused by this daily movement? How are the problems solved?

Japan: the country and its people

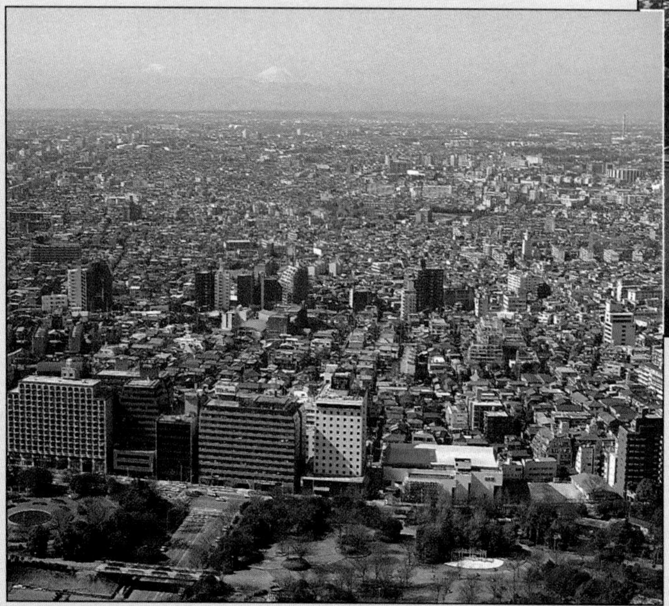

Source A City life, Tokyo's skyline

Source B Rural life, Niigata, the west coast of Japan

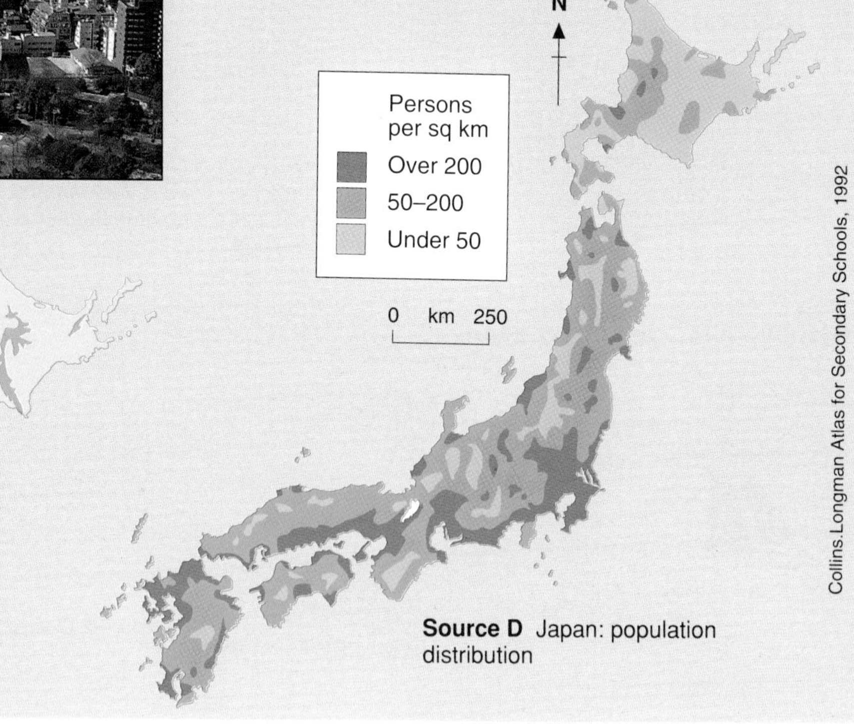

Source D Japan: population distribution

Collins.Longman Atlas for Secondary Schools, 1992

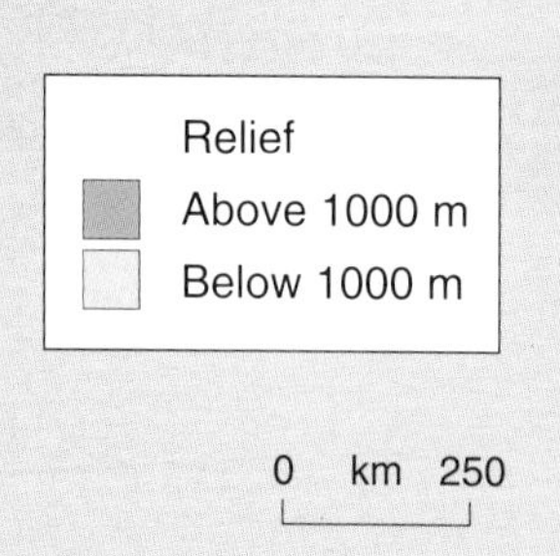

Source C Japan: relief

Ministry of Foreign Affairs, Japan, 1988

1 Study Sources A and B.
a List the differences between the two photographs.
b Give at least one similarity between the photographs.
c Where would you rather live: Tokyo or Niigata? Give reasons.

2 Use an atlas:
a Name the four main islands of Japan.
b Name a major city on each island.
c What is the latitude and longitude of Tokyo, Japan's capital city? Compare this to the latitude and longitude of where you live.

3 **a** Make a tracing of Source C.
b Place your tracing over a copy of Source D.
c Describe the relationship between relief and POPULATION DENSITY.
d Suggest reasons for the relationship you have described.

The Shinkansen

Source E The Shinkansen (bullet train) passes Mount Fuji

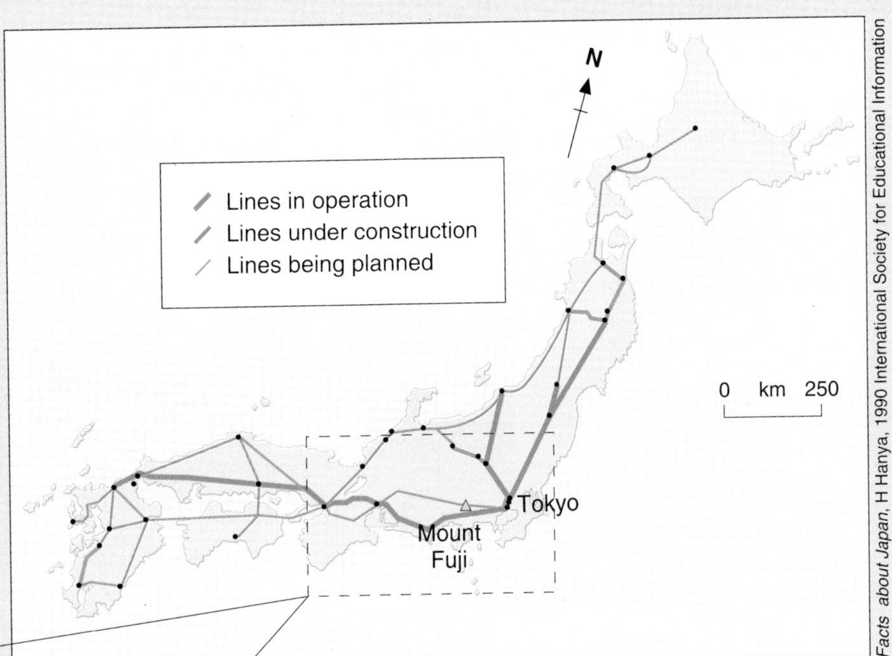

Source F The national Shinkansen network

Facts about Japan, H Hanya, 1990 International Society for Educational Information

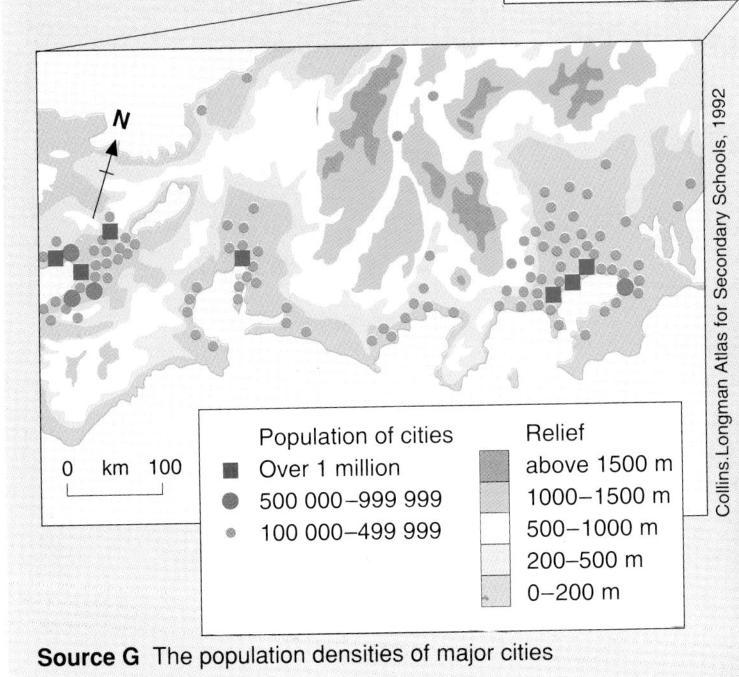

Source G The population densities of major cities

Collins.Longman Atlas for Secondary Schools, 1992

The Tokyo region

Source H A three-tier bus park

4 On Source F, locate where Source E was taken. In which direction was the camera pointing?

5 a Make a tracing of Source F and place it over a copy of Source C.
b Describe and explain the relationship between relief and the Shinkansen network in Japan. Use Source E to help you.
c Place your tracing over Source D. Describe the relationship between population density and the Shinkansen routes.
d Comment on the impact of relief and population density on railway development.
e *Use the* BETA INDEX *to work out whether the Shinkansen network will improve when the planned lines are completed. The higher the Beta Index, the better connected and more developed a transport network is. (The Beta Index is the number of links (rail lines) divided by the number of nodes (places where lines meet).)*

6 Study Source G. Describe the population density of the Tokyo region.

7 Seventy-five million journeys are made daily in the Tokyo region, 99 per cent within the capital.
a How does this affect: • people who travel, • roads and railways?
b Study Source H. Why do you think this is necessary?

11·2 Commuting to Tokyo

Cars and trains

Central Tokyo

Farmland, Chiba district

I travel into Tokyo every weekday to work. I work in an office block in the CENTRAL BUSINESS DISTRICT *(CBD) close to Shinjuku. In central Tokyo there are 70 000 employees per square kilometre. Land prices and housing costs are high. A small apartment within 20 to 30 minutes' travel time of the CBD costs about £1.3 million. My salary, as Branch Office Manager, is £46 000 per annum. I cannot afford these house prices, so I live further away in Aikawa, Kanagawa district.*

I travel into work by car and train. My car journey takes about 30 minutes and the train journey 45 minutes.

Source A Machiko Muto describes her journey to work

I work in an insurance office in Central Tokyo. I live with my parents on the other side of Tokyo Bay in Obitsu, Chiba district. My parents own a farm, but it is too small for all the family to make a living. I enjoy living in the countryside and do not want to move closer to the city.

I travel to work by train. My journey takes about one and a half hours.

Source B Hiroshi Yamada describes his journey to work

Source C Tokyo commuter land

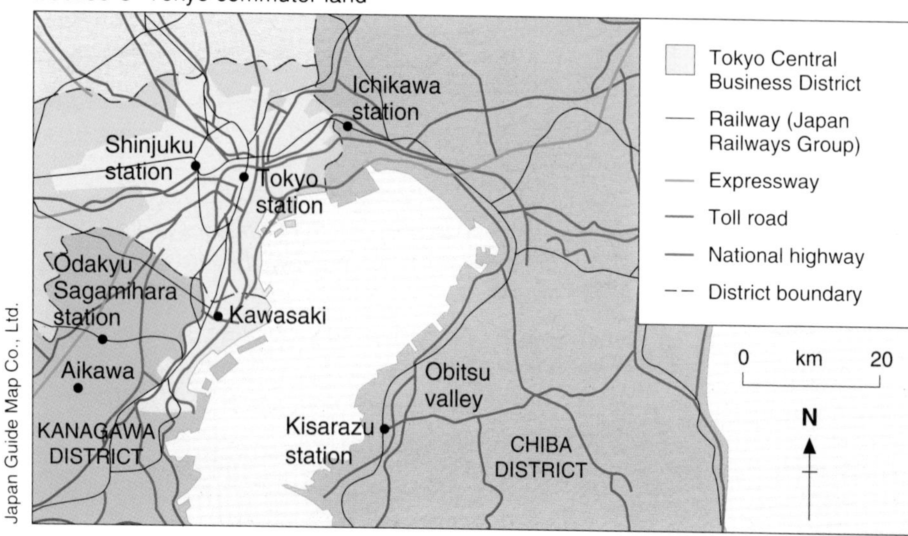

1 Study Source A.

a Describe Tokyo's CBD.

b Suggest reasons why people live some distance from their workplace.

2 Study Sources A, B and C.

a Compare the length of Machiko's and Hiroshi's journeys in terms of:

- travelling time, • distance travelled.

b Work out the average speed of each of their journeys.

c Give reasons for any difference between the average speeds.

d Draw time–distance maps of the two journeys.

Traffic congestion

Sometimes my journey takes longer than one hour and fifteen minutes. I can get caught up in terrible traffic jams. Many busy road junctions are blocked by on-street parking. It is forbidden, but in the city there can be 200 000 illegally parked vehicles during peak times! When traffic is moving, it moves very slowly. Exhaust fumes can be choking, particularly on hot summer days.

Source D Commuting by car

I get a lift with a friend to Kisarazu station. The Limited Express train takes just over an hour to get to Tokyo from Kisarazu. This journey is comfortable but expensive. Express trains are cheaper, but take half an hour longer. Unfortunately, there is not a Shinkansen line from Chiba district.

Source E Commuting by rail

A traffic warden directs the removal of an illegally parked car

3 Study Sources A and D. List the advantages and disadvantages of commuting part of the way to Tokyo by car. Include ideas about cost, time and convenience.

4 Study Sources B and E. Similarly, list the advantages and disadvantages of commuting to Tokyo by rail.

5 Hiroshi is thinking of buying a car and driving to Ichikawa station. He would catch the train to Tokyo from there. Do you consider this would be a wise decision? Justify your answer.

6 Study Source F.
a Copy and complete the table below.

Type of transport	1968 (%)	1988 (%)	Change (%)
Foot	42.9	27.1	–15.8
Motorcycle/bicycle			
Car			
Bus			
Train			

b Which of these changes may have increased traffic congestion in Tokyo today? Explain your answer.

7 *a You are the spokesperson for a group of Tokyo commuters. Make a list of the requests you will send to the city council.*
b Write the city council's reply.

Commuting by Shinkansen

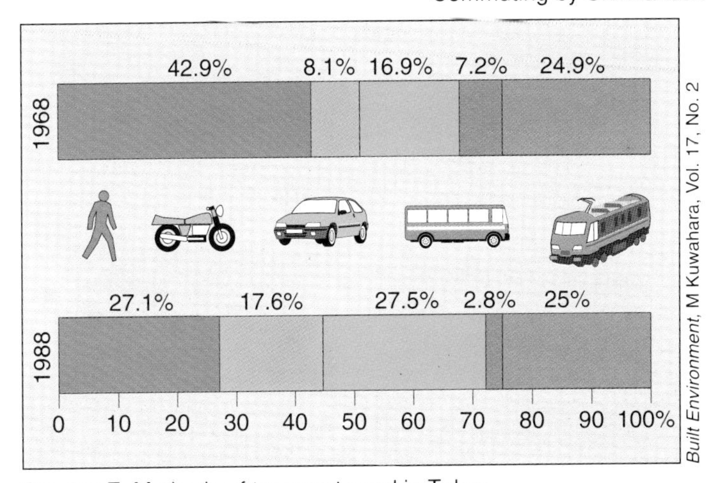

Source F Methods of transport used in Tokyo

Problems on the roads

Year	No. car passengers (% domestic passenger transport)
1960	12
1968	16.8
1970	19.5
1980	39.1
1990	45.6

Source A Car usage in Japan

Facts about Japan, H Harauya, 1990, International Society for Educational Information and *Built Environment*, Vol 17, No 2

Region	1980 km/h	1985 km/h
Tokyo	21	15
Osaka	22	19
Nagoya	26	19
National average	39	37

Source B Peak hour travel speeds on national highways, Japan

Built Environment, Vol 17, No 2

Source C A congested road in Tokyo

By 1987, motorcycle fatality rates in Japan were three times higher than those of other road users; deaths of riders under the age of 24 have been increasing.

The most serious air pollution problem in Tokyo is the emission of nitrogen oxides (NOx); in the city region 70 per cent comes from motor vehicles, of which 71 per cent is from commercial vehicles. Diesel trucks in particular create noise and smoke, as well as NOx pollution.

Although the air quality standards for carbon monoxide (CO) and sulphur dioxide (SO_2) have been met, the NOx standard has not. Only 10 per cent of air monitoring stations show NOx concentrations below the required standard.

1 Study Source A.

a Draw a line graph to show car usage in Japan between 1960 and 1990.

b Describe the link between your graph and Source C.

2 Use Sources A, B, C and D to list at least four problems caused by road traffic in the Tokyo area. Explain how each of the problems affects people in the city.

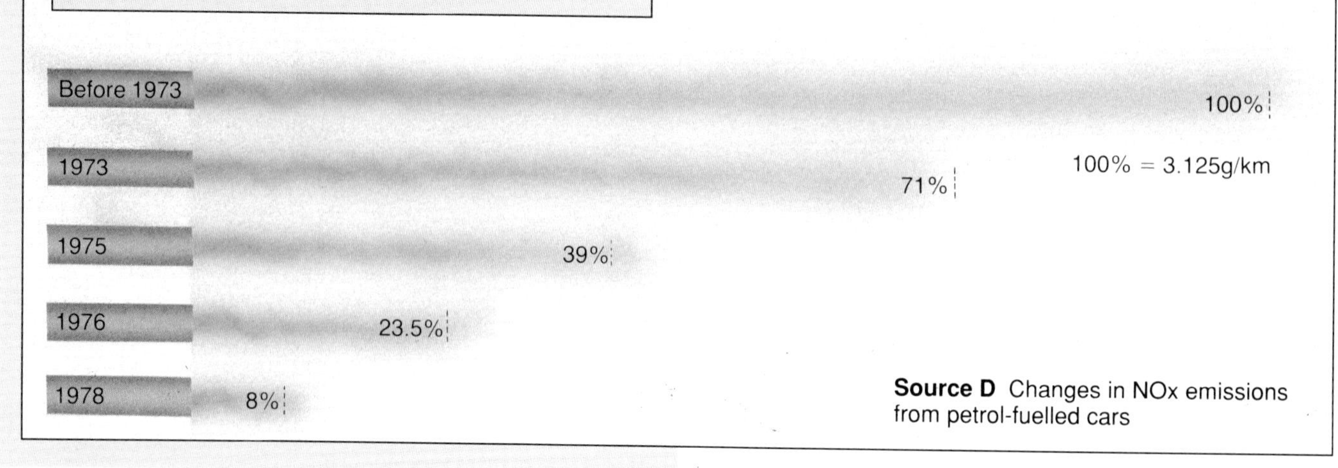

Source D Changes in NOx emissions from petrol-fuelled cars

Environment Agency Government of Japan, 1990

SAITAMA DISTRICT
Outer-ring route
N
CHIBA DISTRICT
Middle-ring route
Inner-ring route
Tokyo
0 km 10
Tokyo Bay
NAGAWA STRICT
— Roads under construction
— Expressway
— Toll road
— National highway
-- District boundary

Built Environment, Vol. 17, No. 2

Source E The road network in the city region, Tokyo

Type of road	Road length (km)	Percentage total network
Intercity expressway	177	0.14
Metropolitan expressway	217	0.17
National highway	2402	1.86
District road	8530	6.59
Local road	118051	91.24

Ministry of Construction (1990) Annual Report of Road Statistics in *Built Environment* Vol 17, No 2

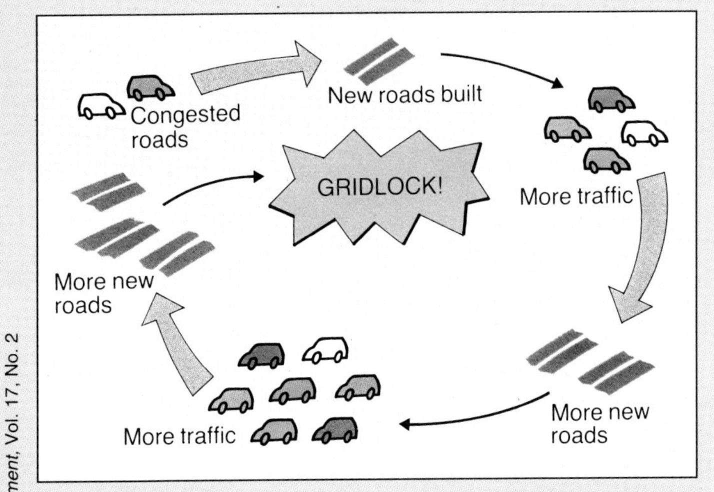

Source F Gridlock!

Source G Toll road

Roads in Japan are publicly owned. They are financed by central government, local government and from special taxes. It costs over £83 million to build one kilometre of expressway. In Tokyo, 12–14 per cent of the land is given over to roads, compared with over 20 per cent for many other world cities.

Any solutions?

Build more roads!

A middle-ring road is being built (Source E) and an outer-ring road has been planned. These roads are intended to reduce congestion, especially at junctions on the inner-ring route.

Make them pay!

Drivers pay a toll (fee) for using expressways (Source G). There are also taxes on petrol and diesel. This money helps to pay for road improvements. If the cost of using private vehicles goes up, it may make people change to other forms of transport.

Other solutions

- Force people by law to change to electric vehicles (slower but quieter and cleaner).
- Close the roads to traffic at certain times.
- Install computer technology to keep traffic flowing smoothly.
- Change working hours to reduce congestion at peak times.

3 Study Source E. Describe the road network in the city region using the words 'ring', 'radial' and 'coastal'.

4 Work in pairs. Study Sources E and F. One solution to the road traffic problem is to build more roads. Discuss whether you think this is a good solution. Give reasons for your views.

5 **a** For each of the given solutions to the road traffic problem, suggest advantages and disadvantages for the road user.
b Rank the solutions, starting with the one that suits the road user best.

6 *'Problems caused by technology can only be solved by technology.' Do you agree? Write a report for the Minister of Transport in Japan.*

11·4 Railway traffic

Problems on the railways

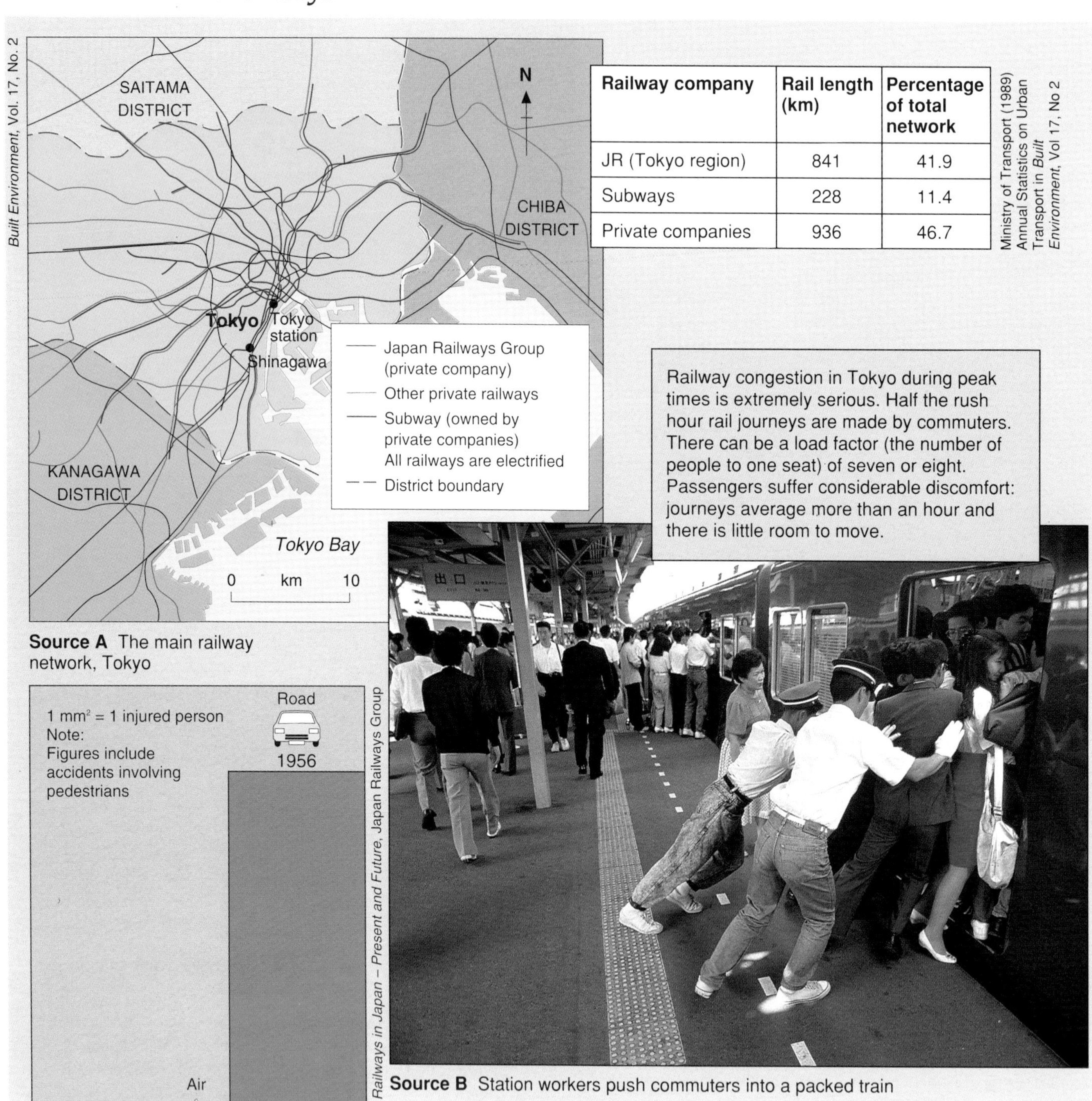

Built Environment, Vol. 17, No. 2

Source A The main railway network, Tokyo

Railway company	Rail length (km)	Percentage of total network
JR (Tokyo region)	841	41.9
Subways	228	11.4
Private companies	936	46.7

Ministry of Transport (1989) Annual Statistics on Urban Transport in *Built Environment*, Vol 17, No 2

Railway congestion in Tokyo during peak times is extremely serious. Half the rush hour rail journeys are made by commuters. There can be a load factor (the number of people to one seat) of seven or eight. Passengers suffer considerable discomfort: journeys average more than an hour and there is little room to move.

Source B Station workers push commuters into a packed train

1 mm² = 1 injured person
Note:
Figures include accidents involving pedestrians

Shinkansen	Conventional rail	Air	Road
0	8	96	1956

High Speed Railways in Japan – Present and Future, Japan Railways Group

Source C Safety comparison of major transport types

1 Study Source A. Describe the railway network using the words 'ring', 'radial' and 'coastal'. How does it compare to the road network (Source E, page 85)?

2 Study Sources A, B and C.
a List the main problems caused by railway traffic in the city region.
b Compare the advantages and disadvantages of Tokyo's road and rail traffic under the headings 'congestion', 'pollution' and 'safety'. Add any other advantages and disadvantages you can think of.

Japan's national railway lines were privatised in 1987. They form the basic network structure, together with other private railways. Subways generally pass below Tokyo's CBD. They are owned by two different organisations. All these railways make most of their money from passenger fares.

Any solutions?

Build more railways!

The Ministry of Transport has plans to reduce the load factor on the railways from seven or eight passengers to four. However, building new lines is as expensive as building expressways: the Hanzomon line cost about £108 million per kilometre. Also, because the subway network is already dense, new lines must be built deep underground.

It is difficult for the private railway companies to raise funds for building new lines because the Japanese government does not give large grants for railway investment, especially in cities. The Government also keeps a limit on fare increases. The railway companies have to choose where to invest and only the Japan Railways Group (JR) is looking to modernise its Shinkansen lines because of competition with domestic airlines.

Build better trains!

There is nothing new about high-speed super-trains. France and Germany have developed trains with a top speed of 406 km/h. These trains run every hour on special tracks. However, in Japan the Shinkansen runs every four minutes, on some lines, at peak times on ordinary track. How can it be improved?

3 Read the above information and look back to page 85. What are the advantages and disadvantages of improving: • the rail network, • the road network? What do you think is the best solution?

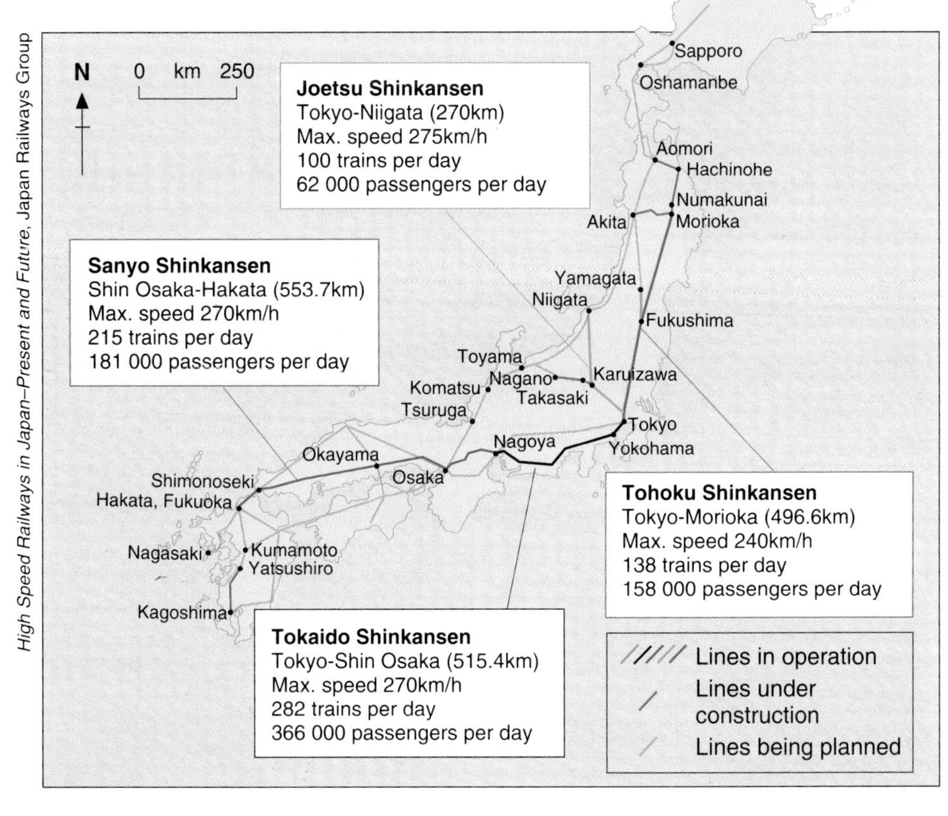

Source E The Shinkansen network

Shinkansen uses:
- one-third the energy consumption of jet aircraft
- one-quarter the energy consumption of motor cars

Source D Work continues in order to improve the Shinkansen

4 Explain why the Shinkansen is not as fast as French and German trains.

5 The Shinkansen should be renamed 'The Shrinkansen'.

a Place a piece of tracing paper over Source E. Mark and name the positions of Tokyo and Osaka. Write 1950 next to Osaka. Draw a straight line between the two places.

b Between 1950 and 1964 journey times between the two cities had reduced from 8 hours to 4 hours. Place a new mark for Osaka halfway along the line to Tokyo. Label it 1964.

c In 1992 the journey time had reduced to 2 hours 30 minutes. Put a mark on the line three-tenths distance from Tokyo to Osaka. Label it 1992.

d Do the same for journeys between:
- Tokyo and Morioka
- Tokyo and Niigata
- Osaka and Hakata.

Assume similar time savings to those made between Tokyo and Osaka.

e Do you agree with the statement which opens this question? Explain your answer.

6 *The Shinkansen is in competition with domestic airlines.*

a *Suggest advantages and disadvantages of both forms of transport to commuters.*

d *Which form of transport would you use and why?*

12·1 URBANISATION – ROOM TO SPARE?

Many millions of people throughout the world live in or around urban areas. These areas are growing in size and number. Why is this happening? What is the impact? How is urban change managed?

Source A
Contrasts in housing

New shopping complex opens on greenfield site

THE GOVERNMENT BLAMES RURAL MIGRANTS FOR SQUATTER SETTLEMENT PROBLEMS

US companies relocate to Mexican border cities

BRITAIN TO PROVIDE SANCTUARY FOR BOSNIAN REFUGEES

Farmers forced to leave traditional homelands

GO-AHEAD GIVEN FOR NEW ESTATE ON URBAN FRINGE

New motorway expected to bring industry and housing to North Yorkshire

New capital city attracts industry and workers

PLANNING PERMISSION GIVEN FOR NEW TOWN

Source B Reasons for growth?

1 Study Source A.
a Describe the different types of land use shown.
b In which housing area would you:
• most like to live, • least like to live?
Give reasons to explain your answers.
c Suggest where this urban area might be.
d Compare your answer with those of other students and explain your choices. Ask your teachers what they think.

2 **a** Use Source B to make a list of reasons which might explain the growth of urban areas.
b Add any other reasons that you can think of. Look back at earlier units for help.
c Choose one of the reasons from your list. Draw a diagram, cartoon or storyboard to show: • how it causes urban growth, • the impact it has.

Patterns of urbanisation

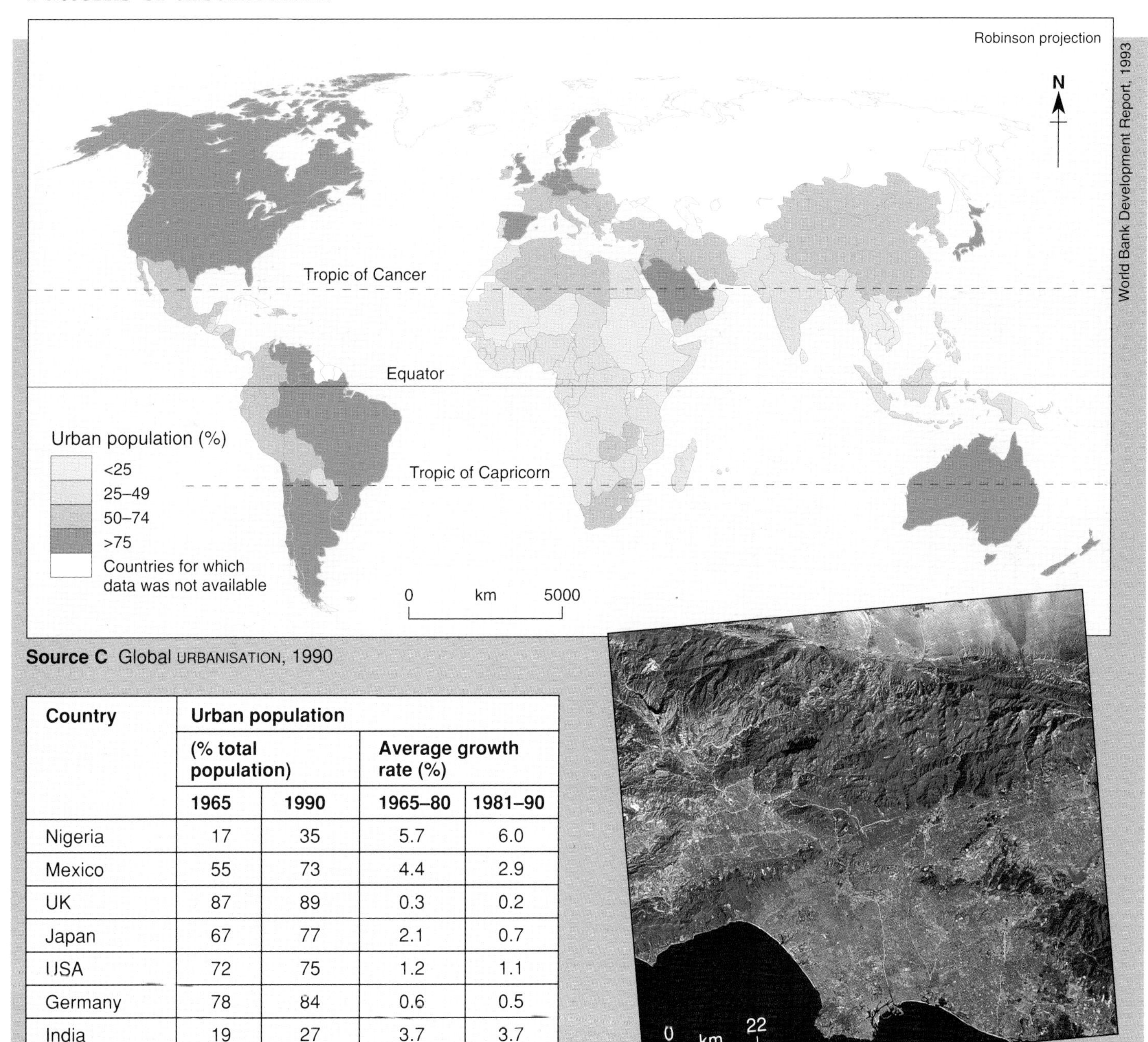

Source C Global URBANISATION, 1990

Country	Urban population			
	(% total population)		Average growth rate (%)	
	1965	1990	1965–80	1981–90
Nigeria	17	35	5.7	6.0
Mexico	55	73	4.4	2.9
UK	87	89	0.3	0.2
Japan	67	77	2.1	0.7
USA	72	75	1.2	1.1
Germany	78	84	0.6	0.5
India	19	27	3.7	3.7
Brazil	50	75	4.3	3.4

Source D The urban population of selected countries

Source E Los Angeles: 2867 people per square kilometre

3 Use Source C and an atlas.
a Name four countries with:
- a high percentage of urban dwellers
- a low percentage of urban dwellers.

b Describe the distribution of countries with:
- a high urban percentage
- a low urban percentage.

c Suggest reasons to explain the patterns you have identified.
d Look back to Source F, page 5. The population of area Z is growing faster than area Y. What impact might this have on the patterns of urban population?

4 Study Source D.
a Draw a bar graph to show how the percentage population in urban areas, for each country, has changed between 1965 and 1990.
b Which countries had the: • highest, • lowest average growth rates between 1981 and 1990? Suggest reasons to explain your answers.
c Describe and explain the trends in average growth rates for 1965–90.

5 Study Source E.
a Use the scale to calculate the area of urban land (blue-grey in colour).
b Estimate how many people live in Los Angeles by multiplying your answer to **a** by the POPULATION DENSITY.
c Use evidence from Source E to explain the location of Los Angeles.
d Make a list of the possible advantages and disadvantages of living in such a large urban area.

The benefits of urban life

Source A The bright lights of New York

Source B Beijing: the industrial outskirts

In many countries throughout the world, urban areas have expanded as a result of the PUSH and PULL FACTORS created by economic growth. If industry is concentrated in an urban area, this can bring benefits. The cost of basic facilities and public services, such as piped water, electricity, education and health care can be reduced. However, differences in culture and wealth mean that not all the population have equal access to these benefits.

Deana Cross at The British Publishing Company Limited, 1992

Source C City services Newcastle-upon-Tyne

Source D The economics of urban growth

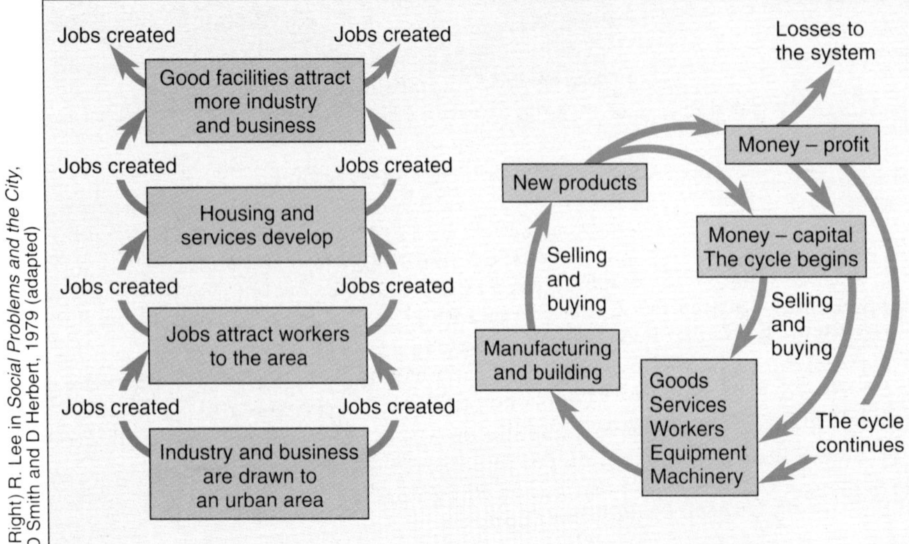

(Right) R. Lee in *Social Problems and the City*, D Smith and D Herbert, 1979 (adapted)

1 Use Sources A, B and C to write about the benefits of living in cities.

2 Study Source D.
a In pairs, discuss possible weaknesses in the economic system and where waste (losses to the system) might occur.
b Use evidence from Source D to describe the likely impact of a decline in manufacturing on an urban area.

The disadvantages of the city

Source E Sleeping rough in London

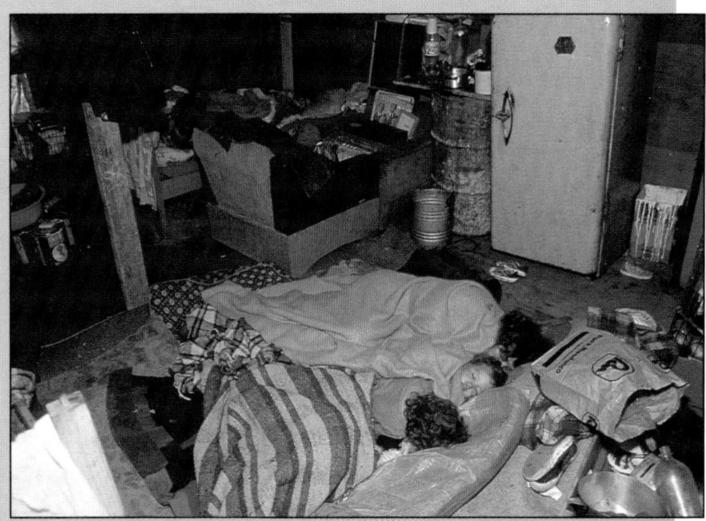

Source F Overcrowding and poverty in São Paulo, Brazil

Source G Demonstrating against cuts to the National Health Service, Manchester

Source H German riot police control protesters against Berlin's bid to host the Olympic Games

BERLIN'S ALEXANDERPLATZ

FRIEDRICH keeps a knife and a tear-gas pistol nearby. 'I need them to protect myself. There's constantly trouble here; the place is always full of trouble-makers. A few weeks ago in Berlin, they murdered a lavatory attendant, just for a few pfennigs.'

Stephan Lebert, *The Guardian*, 16 April 1993

Crime in Turin

LAST year, 30 000 thefts were reported, 82 per day. There were 8000 cars stolen, 3000 cases of pick-pocketing, 880 muggings, 1320 thefts from shops, 2650 burglaries, 11 000 thefts from cars and 900 armed robberies.

Ezio Mascarino, *The Guardian*, 16 April 1993

Source I Troubles in the city

3 Study Sources E, F, G, H and I.

a Note down statements about each source. You could work in a large group:
- Your group should be organised into a circle.
- One person should be the recorder.
- Each person in turn should make one comment about any of the sources. The recorder writes down each statement. If a person does not wish to make a comment, they should say 'pass'. Continue until no more comments are made.

NOTE: Do not comment on what any person says.
- Sort the recorder's list into groups of similar comments.
- Go round the circle again suggesting reasons for the statements that have been listed.

*b Use the statements from **a** to write a report on social problems in cities.*

Urban planning

Town centre to be pedestrianised

Retail park to be built on derelict dockyards

£2 MILLION FACE-LIFT FOR COUNCIL ESTATE

Plans approved for a new inner-ring road

NO NEW DEVELOPMENTS IN GREEN BELT SAY PLANNERS

METROPOLITAN POLICE

NEIGHBOURHOOD WATCH AREA

METROPOLITAN POLICE WE BEAT CRIME TOGETHER NEIGHBOURHOOD WATCH

Source A Urban improvements

The increase in the size and number of urban areas creates challenges for the people who manage them. In most countries throughout the world, it is national and local governments who bear this responsibility. People who make decisions about urban management and development are called PLANNERS.

Cameras focus on falling crime rate

FROM his city centre station, Supt Peter Durham trains the remote camera down a busy shopping street and zooms in on a bus queue. ... with 16 long-range, remote control television cameras monitoring the one square mile centre of Newcastle upon Tyne and taping everything in sight for action replays. At night, infra red scanners light dark alleys.

The system funded by local businesses, the Environment Department and the police authority, was introduced in December ... so far this year had led to an 18 per cent drop in city centre crime ... 'It's the equivalent of having 16 bobbies on the beat around the clock every day of the year,' Supt Durham enthuses.

Keeping a video watch on the streets of Newcastle city centre (above) while one of the cameras surveys the streets (left) which have seen a big fall in crime since they were turned on.

Peter Hetherington, *The Guardian*, 11 July 1993

Source B Reducing crime in Newcastle upon Tyne

1 Using Source A, copy and complete the table for the six urban developments. Try to list two positive effects for each condition.

2 Study Source B.

a Suggest reasons to explain why this scheme was introduced.

b Who might object to such a scheme? List the objections they might have.

c What do *you* think about closed-circuit television keeping an eye on people?

Action	Improvement on:		
	social conditions	economic conditions	environmental conditions
PEDESTRIANISE town centre	More attractive environment	Creates space encourages more shoppers	No traffic reduces noise and air pollution

How to plan

Many urban improvements, such as Newcastle's closed-circuit television system, are solutions to problems resulting from urbanisation. However, some people believe that in order to make our cities better places to live, the causes of problems such as crime, hardship and homelessness need to be tackled. One way this can happen is for politicians and planners to work alongside the people who live in an area: to find out how best to meet local needs and improve the urban environment.

Lea View House

Built in 1939, this five storey, 300 flat estate in Hackney was a typical run-down inner city housing area. Due to increasing building decay and vandalism, community spirit was low and people did not want to live there. In 1980, the council appointed architects, Hunt Thompson Associates, to improve the area. The architects soon realised that, in order to improve the area for the residents, they must involve the residents.

Three months of consultation led to proposals which would transform the area:

- 'Private houses' for large families at ground-floor level.
- Sheltered accommodation for the elderly.
- Flats designed for people with disabilities.
- Tenant involvement with the interior design.

Today, the 'new' estate is complete. The residents have a sense of pride and community spirit. Vandalism, muggings and crime had been virtually eliminated. Fuel bills have been halved, while comfort levels have doubled.

Source C Neighbourhood planning – people as planners, a UK example

Villa el Salvador

Villa el Salvador is Peru's largest pueblo joven

Increasing pressure from rural migrants on the city's resources led to the authorities in Lima, Peru, taking new action. In the past, SQUATTER SETTLEMENTS had been bulldozed and the SQUATTERS moved on. Since the late 1970s, government and local authority planners have worked with residents to design and build new towns or 'pueblos jovenes'. The needs of the squatters are taken into account. Land is used for industry, shops, schools and health clinics. Electricity supplies, domestic water and sewage connections are made to many houses.

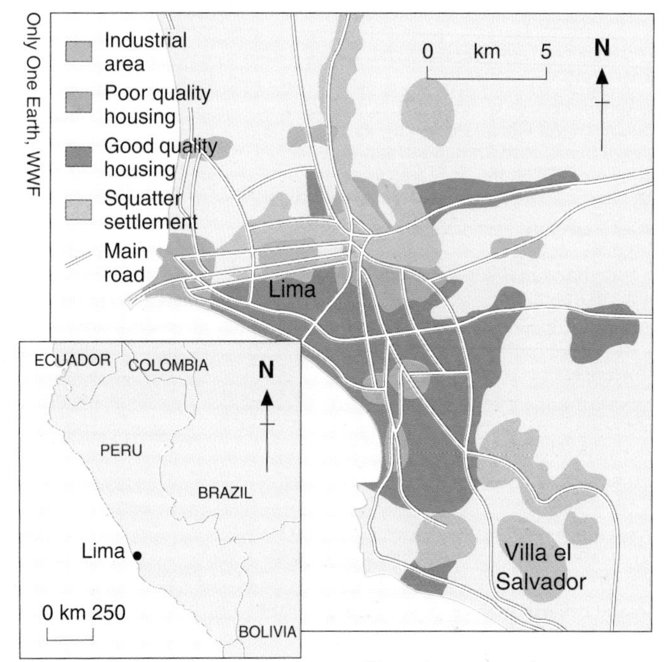

Source D People as planners, a Peruvian example

3 Study Source C. List the likely benefits of the neighbourhood approach to planning.

4 Study Source D.
a How will the action by the city authorities help to improve the QUALITY OF LIFE of the squatters?
b Suggest other things that could be done to help people living in these conditions.

5 *There is a trend for people to move from large towns and cities to seek work and a different quality of life in rural towns and villages. Some people call this process counterurbanisation.*
a Suggest reasons for this movement.
b Describe the possible effects of this movement on village life.
c How is this population movement different to urban growth?

GLOSSARY

ACCESSIBILITY: a measure of the ease and efficiency with which a location can be reached.

BETA INDEX: a measure of accessibility. The number of connections in a network e.g. a road or rail network. Calculated by measuring the number of links, e.g. roads or rail lines, divided by the number of nodes, e.g. road junctions or stations.

BIRTH RATE (CRUDE): the number of live births per 1000 people per year.

BY-PASS: an alternative route for traffic which passes round a settlement. Designed to ease traffic congestion and help traffic flow.

CASH CROP: a crop grown for sale or exchange.

CENSUS: an official population count.

CENTRAL BUSINESS DISTRICT (CBD): the main commercial, shopping and entertainment area of a town or city. It has limited spare space and high land values.

COLONIALISM: settlement of a country, usually through invasion. Rule is exerted over the colonised territory.

COMMUTERS: workers who live some distance from their workplace.

COMPARISON GOODS: goods which are bought infrequently and which are usually expensive, e.g. electrical items. Also known as high-order or luxury goods. Often the price and quality of similar items are compared before being bought.

COMPREHENSIVE REDEVELOPMENT: a policy of clearing low quality housing and rebuilding an area completely in order to create a new, higher quality environment.

CONSUMER GOODS: items bought by individuals for their own needs and enjoyment, e.g. stereos, washing machines, cars.

CONVENIENCE GOODS: items which need to be bought regularly and are usually cheap e.g. groceries, newspapers. Also know as low-order goods.

DEATH RATE (CRUDE): the number of deaths per 1000 people per year.

DISPERSED (SETTLEMENT): buildings which are widely scattered over an area, e.g. a rural area where farms are isolated by farmland.

ECONOMIC DEVELOPMENT: improving the standard of living for the majority of the population. For example, improving housing, health care, access to education and employment opportunities.

EMIGRATION: permanent or semi-permanent migration of individuals or groups from a country. These individuals are known as emigrants.

ENVELOPE SCHEME: a policy for improving low quality housing. Occupants remain in their homes while the repairs are made around them.

ENVIRONMENTAL QUALITY MATRIX: (environmental impact assessment) a method of measuring the quality of an environment. Factors that affect the standard of the environment are graded, e.g. friendliness, litter.

ETHNIC GROUP: a group of people with a shared identity based on common origins or traditions (cultural, national or religious).

ETHNIC MINORITY: ethnic groups who form a small percentage of the total population of an area such as a country.

EUROPEAN COMMUNITY (EC): a group of twelve countries, including the United Kingdom, grouped together for social and economic benefits.

EXPORTS: goods which are produced in one country but sold to another country.

FREIGHT MOVEMENT: the transport of cargo, e.g. by road, rail, sea or air.

GREENFIELD SITE: a site not yet built on.

GROSS DOMESTIC PRODUCT (GDP): the total value of the goods and services produced by a country in a year. It does not include foreign investment.

GROSS NATIONAL PRODUCT (GNP): the total value of goods and services produced by a country in a year. It includes the value of foreign investment. It is one measure of a country's wealth.

'GUESTWORKERS': a term used to describe immigrant workers, often without citizenship, who are employed in a range of low paid jobs. It is particularly used in reference to migrant workers in Germany.

HAMLET: a small group of houses with few or no services. This settlement is not large enough to be called a village.

HIGH-ORDER (GOODS): items which are not bought regularly and are usually expensive. Also known as comparison goods.

HOUSING DENSITY: the average number of homes in each unit of area. The unit of area normally used is a square kilometre.

HOUSING TENURE: the type of legal arrangement held for occupying residential property, e.g. owned, rented.

HUB: the core or centre, from which everything else radiates.

IMMIGRATION: the permanent or semi-permanent migration of individuals or groups into a country. These individuals are known as immigrants.

IMPORTS: goods which are bought from a foreign country.

INFRASTRUCTURE: a system of services which provide a basic framework for an economy, e.g. airports, power supplies, sewage systems.

IRRIGATION: the raising, storage and distribution of water to the land, especially for the growth of food crops.

LAND SPECULATORS: individuals who buy land and then use or sell it for profit.

LOW-ORDER (GOODS): items which are bought regularly and are usually cheap. Also known as convenience goods.

MIGRATION: a permanent or semi-permanent change of residence for an individual. These individuals are known as migrants. The decision to migrate, at any scale, is determined by the balance of push factors, pull factors and other difficulties such as distance, cost, and physical and political barriers.

MOBILITY: the ease by which a person or goods can move from one place to another.

MORTGAGE: a loan, usually from a bank or building society, to buy property.

NATURAL INCREASE: the increase in population due to the difference between birth rate and death rate.

NUCLEATED (SETTLEMENT): a settlement in which the buildings are grouped closely together around a central point or nucleus.

PEDESTRIANISE: to develop an area, from one used by vehicles to one where people are only allowed on foot; other transport is banned.

PERIPHERY: on the edge. Often refers to the edge of a town or city.

PLANNER: a person in authority, who makes decisions about how land is developed in both rural and urban areas.

POPULATION DENSITY: the average number of people living in each unit of area. The unit of area normally used is a square kilometre. This can range from less that one in remote, inhospitable regions, to hundreds in urban areas or on highly productive agricultural land.

PRIMARY PRODUCTS: natural resources produced by primary industry, e.g. fish, farm produce, trees, mined or quarried materials. The output often needs to be processed further.

PULL FACTORS: these are attractive features of a possible future location or place of residence. They could influence an individual's or firm's decision to migrate to the area.

PUSH FACTORS: these are negative features of life at the present location or place of residence. They could influence an individual's or firm's decision to move from the area.

QUALITY OF LIFE: an individual's happiness, satisfaction and social well-being. Features that can affect a person's quality of life include family, housing, income, services.

RANGE: the distance a customer is prepared to travel for a particular item or service.

REFUGEE: a person or group who seeks refuge in another country to escape religious or political persecution in their own country.

SETTLEMENT: a place where people have become established and built homes.

SQUATTER: resident of an area or property to which they have no legal right.

SQUATTER SETTLEMENT: an unplanned residential area, usually on the outskirts of an urban area. It has a high density of low quality homes, built by the occupants from simple materials. The occupants do not own the land and there are often no basic services such as a water supply or sewage system.

SUBSISTENCE FARMING: when a farmer grows food to support the family. In good years some of the extra produce might be sold.

THRESHOLD POPULATION: the smallest number of customers necessary to support a shop or service.

TRIBUTARY: a stream or river which flows into a larger stream or river.

URBANISATION: the process by which there is an increase in the proportion of a country's total population living in urban areas.

INDEX

Published by Collins Educational,
An imprint of HarperCollins*Publishers*,
77-85 Fulham Palace Road,
London W6 8JB

First published 1994
Reprinted 1994

ISBN 0 00 3266540

Outline design by Gill Mouqué
Design by Wendi Watson
Cover design by Jerry Fowler and Chi Leung
Illustrations by Joan Corlass, Jeremy Gower, Douglas Hall, Tonia Thorne
Maps and diagrams by Contour Publishing, Jerry Fowler, Hardlines, Jillian Luff
Picture research by Liz Heasman
Edited by Kate Hardcastle
Production by Fiona Hazard

The authors and publishers are grateful to the following for their comments on the manuscript:
Central Japan Railway Company;
Donald Hinds;
Richard Lawton;
Library, Nigeria High Commission;
Local Studies Centre, Norwich Central Library;
Japan National Tourist Organization.

Typeset by Dorchester Typesetting Group Ltd, Dorchester, Dorset
Printed and bound in Italy by Rotolito Lombarda, Milan

Acknowledgements

Every effort has been made to contact the holders of copyright material, but if any have been inadvertently overlooked the publishers will be pleased to make the necessary arrangements at the first opportunity.

PHOTOGRAPHS The publishers would like to thank the following for permission to reproduce photographs:

Cover photograph of Birmingham New Street. John Birdsall Photography.

Adams Picture Library 21L, 44TL, 51TR&TL, 57R, 65TR&CLT&B;
Carlos Reyes Manzo/APA 93T;
Birmingham City Council 59CL&B, 71TR;
By permission of Birmingham Library Services 60B;
Cambridge University Collection of Air Photographs: copyright reserved 64R;
J. Allan Cash Ltd. 7T, 13TR, 23B, 28BL, 29, 34TL&TC&B, 35, 36, 37BR, 38R, 39B, 41T;
Central Japan Railway Company 87;
Prodeepta Das 32T;
Das Photo/David Simpson 13TL&B, 15CL;
Courtesy of the Department of Transport 74L, 76BL&BR;
DPA/PA/Kumm 9;
DPA/PA/Witschel 20;
Commission of the European Communities 12T;
European Investment Bank 12R;
European Parliament 12L&C;
Farset Enterprise Park Ltd. 53R;
Robert Harding Picture Library 4B, 5, 8C, 22T, 24, 25TC, 28T, 39T, 40, 80, 81T, 82TC, 83, 90TL&TR;
Kate Harris 32B;
Housing Executive 54, 55;
Geoff Howard 82TR&B, 83CL&CR;
Hunt Thompson Associates 93C&B;
Hutchison Library 7B, 22B, 23TR, 25TL&BL&CR, 31L, 34TR, 39T&C, 41C&B;
Impact Photos/Carolina Salguero 10R;
Impact Photos/Peter Arkell 91TL;
Japan Archive 85;
Claire Jones 28BR;
Linen Hall Library 52TC;
Manchester Airport 33;
Thomas Hoepker/Magnum Photos 14CL;
Gilles Peress/Magnum Photos 19;
Bruno Barbey/Magnum Photos 84;
Adrian Meredith Photography/British Airways 57L;
C.S.Middleton 42, 43T&B, 44, 45, 47, 48, 49;
John Morris 58, 59TL&TR, 60T, 61, 63, 64L, 68T,70B, 71TL;
NASA 4T;
Mike Goldwater/Network 91TR;
John Sturrock/Network 91CL;
Newcastle Chronicle and Journal 92;
NHPA 76BC;
Nigeria High Commission 31R;
Northern Ireland Tourist Board 51C, 53L;
Pacemaker Press International Ltd. 50T, 51B;
Panos Pictures 23TL, 25BR, 27, 37BL;
Roy Peters Photography 59CR, 62, 65TL, 65CLB&R, 66R, 70T, 71C&B;
Nick Reggler 25CL;
Rex Features Ltd. 8B, 10L, 14TL&CR&B, 18, 38L, 81B, 82TL, 83T, 91CR;
Earth Satellite Corporation/Science Photo Library 89;
Frank Spooner Pictures/Gamma/Shone 8T;
Frank Spooner Pictures/Gamma/Piel 15BL;
Frank Spooner Pictures/Gamma/Merillon 15CR&BR;
Frank Spooner Pictures/Gamma/Bouvet 15TR;
Frank Spooner Pictures/Gamma/Saussier 17, 21R;
Tony Stone Images 4C, 57C, 67, 86, 88;
D.Aubert/Sygma 14TR;
Ulster Folk and Transport Museum (photo: WAG 3734) 52BR;
By kind permission of the Trustees of the Ulster Museum 52TL&BL&BC;
University College Dublin 11;
Unborn child by Gustave Vigland, © DACS 1994 Vigeland-Museet 6;
Simon Warner 72B, 73;
Yorkshire Post 74R, 75, 76T&CL&CR.

T = Top, B = Bottom, C = Centre, L = Left, R = Right.

CENSUS DATA Unit 9 1991 © Crown copyright.

SPEECH Unit 3 Walter Monper, *Europe and German Unification*, R. Fritsch-Bournazel, 1992.

MAPS Page 48TL © Color Maps International
Pages 46 and 77T Reproduced from the 1:50 000 scale Landranger maps with the permission of the Controller of Her Majesty's Stationery Office, © Crown Copyright.
Page 90CR Deana Cross at the British Publishing Company Limited, 1992 ©